The Ioway in Missouri

Project Sponsor

Western Historical Manuscript Collection,
University of Missouri–Columbia

Special Thanks
Missouri State Archives

Missouri Heritage Readers
General Editor, Rebecca B. Schroeder

Each Missouri Heritage Reader explores a particular aspect of the state's rich cultural heritage. Focusing on people, places, historical events, and the details of daily life, these books illustrate the ways in which people from all parts of the world contributed to the development of the state and the region. The books incorporate documentary and oral history, folklore, and informal literature in a way that makes these resources accessible to all Missourians.

Intended primarily for adult new readers, these books will also be invaluable to readers of all ages interested in the cultural and social history of Missouri.

Other Books in the Series

The Ioway in Missouri

Greg Olson

University of Missouri Press   Columbia and London

Copyright © 2008 by
The Curators of the University of Missouri
University of Missouri Press, Columbia, Missouri 65201
Printed and bound in the United States of America
All rights reserved
5 4 3 2 1   12 11 10 09 08

Library of Congress Cataloging-in-Publication Data

Olson, Greg, 1959–
    The Ioway in Missouri / Greg Olson.
        p. cm.
    Includes bibliographical references and index.
    Summary: "Focusing on the Ioways' role in Missouri's colonial and early state-
hood periods, Olson describes Ioway creation stories and oral tradition; farming
and hunting practices; relations with neighboring tribes, incoming white settlers, and the U.S. government; and challenges to their way of life and survival
as a people"—Provided by publisher.
    ISBN 978-0-8262-1824-7 (alk. paper)
    1. Iowa Indians—Missouri—History. 2. Iowa Indians—Missouri—Govern-
ment relations. 3. Indians, Treatment of—Missouri. 4. Missouri—History.
I. Title.
    E99.I6O57 2008
    977.80497'52—dc22
                                        2008025867

Designer: Jennifer Cropp
Typesetter: Foley Design
Printer and binder: Thompson-Shore, Inc.
Typefaces: Palatino and Adobe Garamond

For Chris and Tess

Contents

Acknowledgments

I am indebted to many people and organizations for help and support as I completed this manuscript. I owe Jimm GoodTracks a special note of thanks for opening many doors for me and for providing me with a glimpse of the rich culture and language of the Ioway-Otoe-Missouria people. Without his years of guidance, patience, and generosity, this manuscript would not exist.

I would also like to thank Suzette McCord-Rogers, curator of the Kansas State Historical Society's Native American Heritage Museum, for her helpful suggestions and for introducing me to a number of wonderful and knowledgeable members of the Ioway community. Lynn Alex of the Office of the State Archaeologist in Iowa City, Iowa, was extremely generous in directing me to resources that proved valuable in helping me understand the archaeological history of the Oneota and Ioway. Mike Dickey, site administrator at the Arrow Rock State Historic Site, in Arrow Rock, Missouri, pointed me toward important published resources on early Ioway history, while Alan Perry, formerly an archivist with the National Archives and Records Administration–Kansas City provided valuable research guidance during my visit to NARA. Thanks also to Bill Stolz at the University of Missouri Western Historical Manuscript Collection–Columbia. I wrote this manuscript while I was enrolled in the master's program in the Department of History at the University of Missouri–Columbia. I would like to thank my advisers, Dr. Susan Flader and Dr. Jeffrey Pasley, for their guidance in this endeavor.

I am also indebted to Martha Royce Blaine for her outstanding scholarship on the Ioway people. Her book *The Ioway Indians* served as a guide throughout my research and was instrumental in directing me toward critical primary and secondary sources. I also found valuable resources on the Ioway Cultural Institute Web site created and maintained by Lance Foster.

I want to extend a special note of thanks to Becky Schroeder for convincing me to write this book and for the countless hours she devoted to helping me improve it.

And finally, I would like to express my gratitude to my wife, Christine Montgomery. Aside from her support at home, she readily offered her considerable skills as an editor and image researcher. This project is much better for her efforts. Thank you for your patience through the long process of researching and writing this book. Maybe now we can move the computer out of the living room.

Out of respect for the Ioway tradition, I humbly ask readers to forgive any misinterpretations or misrepresentation of the Ioway people and their culture that my words may suggest.

The State Historical Society of Missouri Richard Brownlee Fund generously underwrote a portion of the research necessary to complete this manuscript. Some sections of the book have previously appeared in the *Missouri Historical Review*.

Notes on Terminology

Readers will notice that I have avoided using the word "chief" in this book. The title does not accurately reflect the role of tribal leaders in traditional Ioway society. "Chief" often refers to a single leader who has sole authority over an entire tribe. In the Ioway tribe several leaders traditionally shared responsibility for governing. It was Europeans and Americans who introduced the idea of recognizing just one individual as the "head chief" of the Ioway nation.

The names of historical American Indian people can cause much confusion for historians. Ioway people often received several names over the course of their lives. A single person might have a birth name, a clan name, a name related to a good deed or act of bravery, and a French, Spanish, or English name used by European or American acquaintances and government officials. In some cases native people could be commonly known by two or more of these names at one time. For example, the Ioway headman White Cloud was also commonly known to European Americans as Mahaska. This is an Americanization of the Baxoje-Jiwere language pronunciation of his name, MaxúThka: *Maxú* meaning Cloud, and *Thka* meaning White. Frontier writers, many of whom struggled to spell correctly in their own language, recorded White Cloud's Baxoje name in letters and documents as Mak-hos-kah, Ma-has-kah, Mash Ka Ka hi, Man-hoo-shaw, and Macha Karres.

In some cases, Indian people changed their common names over the course of time. The Ioway headman Great Walker was known as Big Neck toward the end of his life. This name change probably came as the result of an important event or personal accomplishment. When several names are used for a single person, it can be difficult to correctly identify that individual in historical documents. For reasons of simplicity, I refer to Ioway individuals who appear in this book by English (and occasionally French and Spanish) translations of their names. In most cases, these were the names most commonly used by the European and American people who knew them, and it is the way they are identified in historical documents. I have also included the Baxoje names of Ioway individuals. The Ioway-Otoe-Missouria language words and names used in this book have been generously provided by Jimm GoodTracks, author of *Ioway-Otoe-Missouria Nations' Language Study Books* and a dictionary of the Baxoje-Jiwere language.

When mentioning various Indian tribes in this book I have used the tribal names and spellings each tribe prefers today, using outdated tribal names and spellings only when they are part of a quote.

The Ioway in Missouri

Introduction

The White People . . . they made the animals, the birds,
everything disappear. Because of all of this, it can never
be today the way it used to be, when we moved around
. . . we will never again be that way.

— Robert Small, 1936

One morning in April 1842, as the Reverend Samuel Irvin
walked to an Ioway village on the Great Nemaha Reservation in
present-day northeast Kansas, he received a dire warning. An
old Ioway man met him outside the village and begged him not
to continue or he might cross paths with Little Spotted Bear, a
grieving Ioway man whose child had recently died. The old
man feared for Reverend Irvin's safety because Little Spotted
Bear had reportedly vowed to kill a *Ma'unke,* or white man. In
his grief for the loss of his child and his anguish over the suffering his people had long endured, Little Spotted Bear had declared, according to the old man, that "the Ioways were dying
off anyhow . . . he would kill a white man and then the Ioways
would be killed off quick, which would be very good." For the
grieving Ioway father, the rapid death of his people at the hands
of federal troops was preferable to the slow death by starvation
he feared on the reservation.

1

This heartbreaking incident is just one of many recorded by Reverend Irvin while he lived among the Ioway between 1841 and 1848. As he instructed Ioway children in English and ministered to the sick and needy, Irvin despaired at the poverty, alcoholism, and overall "wretched conditions" he found on the reservation. "They seem to be grow[ing] worse and worse," Irvin wrote in February 1841. "I cannot conjecture where it will end."

Irvin's stories illustrate the extreme economic, spiritual, and psychological desperation that marked the lives of the Ioway during their first decade on the reservation. For the Ioway, the Great Nemaha Reservation, where the U.S. government resettled them in 1837, was a foreign land. There ÑiShoje, the smoky water that the whites called the Missouri River, separated them from their homeland, which was now lost to land-hungry white settlers.

Their new home was far from their traditional territory and the bones of their ancestors. Their small reservation provided little opportunity for the Ioway to follow the traditional lifestyle that had supported them for centuries. Within a few short years after their arrival, the animals on which they depended for food and clothing, such as the buffalo and the beaver, began to disappear. In order to survive, some Ioway followed the advice of Reverend Irvin and the U.S. government's Indian agents, and learned to weave their own cloth, raise cattle, and grow corn on square plots of plowed land as their white neighbors did. But many of them were still forced to rely on the government annuities they received as payment for their former homeland east of the Missouri River.

Surviving had not always been so difficult for the Ioway. During the 1840s, older members of the tribe remembered a time just two generations earlier when their lives had been far different. Before the beginning of the nineteenth century, the Ioway enjoyed a vibrant culture. They were excellent farmers and grew fields of corn, squash, and beans in the fertile river bottoms near their villages. They hunted in the river valleys that surrounded their villages and on the prairies far to the west where they pursued *che,* the buffalo. Their skill in hunting allowed them to participate in an active trade economy with neighboring tribes and with the French, Spanish, and British. In those days, European traders traveled the rivers, eagerly exchanging their metal manufactured goods with the Ioway for the furs of animals, especially that of *thinye braxge,* the beaver.

The Ioways' military power was so strong at the beginning of the nineteenth century that the Ioway headman known as the Orator boasted years later that no other Indian nation had dared to build a fire or make a moccasin track between the Missouri and Mississippi Rivers without the Ioways' permission. Perhaps most important, the Ioway were supported physically and spiritually by a way of life that followed the annual rhythms of the earth and connected them to the other beings that shared the earth with them.

Yet, in four short decades, this lifestyle had been nearly destroyed. How had the near destruction of Ioway culture and the Ioway people come about so quickly? This book tries to answer that question. America's westward expansion in the nineteenth century is often told as a series of dramatic battles between the United States and the Indians. In that story, European Americans conquered the West by overpowering native peoples in a series of terrible military defeats. Historians now realize, however, that the truth is much more complicated. The Ioway, like many other Indian nations, never directly engaged in armed conflict with the U.S. military. There is no decisive battle or single tragic event that will easily explain their tragic decline.

Many forces shaped the extreme challenges the Ioway people experienced in the face of white settlement between 1800 and 1838. Their struggle was part of a larger shift in economics, environment, and culture that European and American settlers brought with them when they began moving into the Ioways' homeland. For a time, the Ioway were able to live side by side with the settlers while maintaining their own way of life. By the

1820s, however, the settlers had become so numerous that the Ioways' lives were drastically reshaped by the rapidly changing world around them.

The Ioway, like many other Indian nations that lived along the Missouri and Mississippi Rivers, were not always helpless victims in this changing world. In order to survive, they made difficult choices. At various times their decisions led them to ally with neighboring Indian tribes, incoming settlers, and the U.S. government. At other times, they chose to act forcefully and violently against these same groups. The path to survival was uncertain and the Ioway did not always agree among themselves on the direction they should take as they struggled to meet the new challenges of a changing world.

1

Continuing in the Spirit of that First Meeting between the Bear and the Buffalo

There is ample historical evidence that the Ioway had settled in present-day Missouri by the end of the eighteenth century. At least one map drawn by an unknown French mapmaker shows that some Ioway people may have lived near the Grand River, in north-central Missouri, as early as the 1740s. However, archaeologists believe that some of the Ioways' ancestors, known as the Oneota people, lived in northern Missouri even before Europeans arrived in North America. Archaeological digs along the Chariton, Grand, and Missouri Rivers show that some Oneota people built villages there as early as the twelfth and thirteenth centuries. Though these ancestors of the Ioway left behind stone chips, animal bones, and pieces of pottery that give us hints about their lifestyle, we still know little about them.

Archaeologists debate about where and how the Oneota people lived in the centuries before they arrived in present-day Missouri. Both traditional stories and archaeological evidence indicate that they once lived in a place they call *Maya^{n}Shuje*, or Red Earth, in the region of the upper Mississippi River valley and the Great Lakes. The Oneota included the Ioways' closest

Siouan-speaking relatives, the Winnebago, Otoe, and Missouria tribes, and they seem to have developed their own culture between 950 and 1150 A.D. while the great mound city of Cahokia, near present-day St. Louis, was still active. It is unclear whether the early Oneota were part of the same Mississippian culture that lived at Cahokia, but it seems that the two groups were in contact with one another.

Evidence suggests that between the twelfth and the sixteenth centuries the Oneota spread into what is now Illinois, Indiana, Iowa, and Minnesota. It was during this migration that archaeologists believe the Oneota first settled in northern portions of present-day Missouri. This mass relocation may have been due to a combination of climatic changes, European diseases, and the depletion of large animal populations. After 1500, Indian people contracted diseases such as smallpox, measles, and influenza as the tragic results of the arrival of Europeans on the North American continent. The foreign diseases spread quickly and widely through native populations, often well in advance of European exploration and settlement of the continent. The high death rate among native people forced survivors to regroup into smaller tribal bands that spread out in order to support themselves.

As the Ioway began to identify themselves as a separate group, they called themselves *Báxoje,* which means "gray snow" in the language they shared with the Otoe and Missouria people. This name originated outside the tribe. Some say that their close relatives, the Otoe, gave them this name one winter when they saw that the snow covering the Ioways' lodges had turned gray from the ash of their fires. Others say that the name can be translated as "dusty noses," and according to this story, the name comes from a time long ago when the Ioway located their camp on a sandbar in a river. The blowing wind covered their faces with fine dust, causing visitors to the camp to refer to the tribe by that name.

The Ioways' neighbors, the Dakota, referred to them as *Ayúxba,* which, according to archaeologist Mildred Mott Wedel, means "dusty heads," but others have translated this word to mean "those broken off," in reference to their separation from their Siouan relatives. In the language of the Ioways' Algonquian-speaking neighbors to the east, the Illinois and the Sac and Fox, the word *Ayúxba* was pronounced "Ayuway." The French, who first learned about the Ioway from these Algonquin-speaking people, referred to them by their own variation of that name, *Aiaouez*. Over time, the spelling was standardized into the name we know them by today, Ioway.

Traditional Ioway culture is rooted in the tribe's understanding of their place in the natural world. Their traditional creation stories tell how the Ioway came from mother earth and the sky and explain how they were related to the four-legged animals and winged birds. An important part of Ioway life was devoted to maintaining their kinship ties with the earth and their animal relatives. This kinship can be seen in the Ioway language, in which the word for "being," *wan^shige,* is used when speaking about both humans and animals. Traditional Ioway people continue to believe that there are many different *wan^shige* in the world, and that all have a purpose and all are equal to one another.

According to the Ioways' oral tradition, a variety of animals and birds lived in the world soon after its creation. Whether large or small, all of these beings were able to communicate with one another. Even after some of the animals changed themselves into humans, they retained some animal characteristics and continued to communicate with their nonhuman relatives.

Oral tradition explains how the Ioway clan ancestors descended from these early human beings and were divided into two groups. The Sky People arrived on earth from a world above while the Earth People emerged from a world below the earth. In their wanderings, the Earth People, led by four Bear Brothers, met the four Buffalo Brothers who led the Sky People. They all sat together in a council in which they shared their sacred pipes and decided to become one people, the Ioway.

Both the Sky and Earth People established various clans. The Sky People were made up of the Buffalo, Owl, and Wild Pigeon clans while the Earth People included the Bear, Elk, Eagle, Wolf, and Beaver clans. Many of these Ioway clans continue today. In the spirit of that first meeting between the Buffalo and Bear ancestors, the two clans that carried their names shared leadership responsibility for the Ioway people. In the fall, the sound of the elk's mating whistle was the signal that it was time for the Bear clan to govern the tribe. They led the Ioway throughout the fall and winter as that was the season, according to oral tradition, they emerged upon the earth. In the spring the Buffalo clan assumed the responsibility of tribal leadership at the first sound of the small green tree frogs.

The way in which the Ioway set up their camps demonstrated this balance of power between the Bear and Buffalo clans. They divided their camp circle into two halves: one half was occupied by the lodges of members of the Sky clans, led by the Buffalo clan, and the other half by those belonging to members of the Earth clans, led by the Bear clan. To ensure that family ties continued between all clans, members of the tribe were forbidden from marrying anyone belonging to their own clan or their mother's clan.

The leader of either the Bear or the Buffalo clan directed civic affairs and community ceremonies of all the Ioway during the six months that his clan governed the tribe. While this principal headman was responsible for decisions related to the tribe's affairs, his power was far from absolute. He was guided in his decision-making by the opinions expressed in a council that was made up of the leaders of each of the clans. No decision was considered final as long as members of the council challenged it. The positions of the clan leaders and principal headmen were hereditary. Upon the death of a headman, his eldest living son filled his spot. If a leader had no sons, the son of a daughter or the son of a niece could succeed him. Ioway women were never allowed to hold the position of headman.

A different set of headmen provided leadership in the military affairs of the Ioway. These men were the keepers of the war bundles of the various clans. When a warrior wanted to raise a war party he had to first consult these military headmen, who then met in council with the members of the war party to help them prepare for battle with the proper songs, prayers, dances, and purification ceremonies. It was also the responsibility of the military headmen to receive visitors into Ioway villages and ensure the safety of the visitors during their stay. These visits were an important part of creating and maintaining peaceful intertribal relations and alliances.

The form of the Ioways' civic and military government reflected a vision that sought to maintain a balance between opposing forces. This balance can be found in nature, where summer is always followed by winter, and the sky is in balance with the earth. Accordingly, the Ioway people valued the importance of living in a way that maintained the balance of natural, spiritual, and personal forces. By dividing the leadership of the tribe equally between two clans, and spreading the responsibilities of leadership among a number of different civic and military leaders, the Ioway sought to maintain balance in their social organization as well.

The Ioway usually located their permanent villages in the wooded valleys near large rivers. Easy access to major waterways was critical for transportation and trade, and the river bottomland provided good hunting and excellent soil for crops. The villages were located on terraces just above the bottomland, or in some cases on river bluffs. The Ioway built various types of lodges. Their most permanent dwellings were made of large slabs of walnut or elm bark layered over a wooden frame. These lodges were large and rectangular in shape—measuring 30 to 40 feet long, 20 feet wide, and 14 feet high at the ridge of their peaked roofs—with one door facing the east and one door facing the west. Other lodges had round, arching roofs and were covered with four layers of large mats made of woven cattails. It was not unusual to have an open-air arbor made of a wooden

crops. In the fall the whistling of the elk announced the beginning of the Bear clan's tribal leadership and the time for the fall buffalo hunt.

The buffalo clearly held an important place in the spiritual and physical lives of the Ioway. According to tradition, their buffalo ancestors had introduced corn to the Ioway. In the spring, no one could plant until the Buffalo clan placed the first seeds of corn in the fields. The Ioway tradition includes stories about the origin of buffalo hunting. One story tells of a race between a horse and a buffalo to see which had the right to hunt the other. The horse won, earning its role in helping the Ioway chase the buffalo in the hunt.

Many members of the tribe helped with the annual buffalo hunts. In fact, so many Ioway men and women traveled west to participate in the hunts that European traders discovered it was profitable for them to follow the tribe to its hunting camps to trade. Even in the days before the Ioway people had horses, they traveled great distances across the prairie to follow the buffalo herds. The French explorer Nicolas Perrot wrote in 1685 that Ioway hunters were skilled at killing buffalo even when pursuing them on foot. The introduction of horses into Ioway life around 1720 not only provided hunters with an advantage in chasing their prey but also made it possible for them to set up their temporary hunting camps hundreds of miles from their permanent villages.

In these camps, the Ioway lived in temporary lodges made of animal hides stretched over willow frames. According to some European observers the Ioway also sometimes lived in teepees covered with buffalo hides. Because hunters could advance as much as ten to twenty miles a day, lodges in hunting camps were small and easy to move. Activities in the camps mainly involved preparing animal hides and smoking and drying buffalo meat.

Strict rules guided the way in which meat was divided between the people who took part in a buffalo hunt. The hunter who brought down a buffalo received its hide, while the rest of the animal was distributed to ensure that everyone on the hunt had meat. The Ioway people used the buffalo's hide, bones, hooves, and horns to make everything from lodge covers to clothing to tools.

The Ioway hunted a variety of other animals to sustain them throughout the year, especially deer, which tended to be plentiful in the wooded river valleys where they located their villages. They also hunted elk for their meat and hides and for their bones and antlers, which they fashioned into hoes and hide scrapers. Less plentiful were bears and wolves, both of which the Ioway prized for their hides.

Even after they had guns, the Ioway preferred to hunt with bows and arrows. Because bows were lighter than guns, they were easier for hunters to carry on horseback. A good hunter could take more shots in less time with a bow and arrow because guns of the period had to be reloaded after each shot. Compared to early firearms, arrows were also far more accurate and efficient in killing large animals like buffalo. Paul Wilhelm, Duke of Wuerttemberg, who met a group of Ioway men traveling on the Missouri River near the present-day town of Rocheport, Missouri, in 1823, was impressed by the elegant craftsmanship of the Ioways' bows. Paul noted that each of the Ioway hunters he met carried about one hundred arrows in a quiver. Although for centuries the Ioway had tipped their arrows with stone points, the arrows Duke Paul saw had metal tips skillfully made from old knife blades and other bits of recycled metal obtained in trade.

Like other tribes, the Ioway traveled widely across the prairie for hunting, trading, war, or simply to visit relatives in other villages. In the centuries before they owned horses, they had gained a reputation for being walkers of great stamina, capable of covering long distances on the many overland foot trails and buffalo paths that crisscrossed the land. The reputation for stamina is evident in the name taken by the nineteenth-century Ioway leader, Great Walker.

The Ioway were also known for their skill in navigating the rivers between the Mississippi, which the Ioway called the

Great Water, *Ñítan,* and the Missouri, which they called *ÑiShoje,* Smoky Water. When Duke Paul encountered a group of Ioway men on the Missouri River in 1823, he commented that their large boats looked like French pirogues. They were made from logs the men carefully hollowed out with hot coals. The Ioways' pirogues could travel separately or tied together in groups. Paul noted that even though the boat he saw was large enough to carry twenty men, it moved "with the swiftness of an arrow." The speed and size of the pirogues played an important role in the ability of the Ioways to transport both large amounts of trade goods and large war parties quickly.

Over the centuries, the Ioway developed a rich and vibrant culture based on the rhythms of the seasons and the natural characteristics of the open prairie and the wooded river valleys in which they lived. The Ioways' day-to-day relationship with mother earth and with their animal relatives defined their culture and their worldview. The Ioway, however, were not alone in their homeland. There were other Indian people—and, later, European immigrants—living near and passing through their land. Trade, councils, or war with their neighbors exposed the people to new ideas, new tools, and new weapons. Over time, the Ioway adopted some of these new goods and ideas for their own use. Though deeply rooted in tradition, the life of the Ioway never stood still. As a result of contact with other groups of people, the Ioway were always evolving and adapting to an ever-changing world.

2

Contact and Exchange

The Ioway were living along the rivers of what is now south-east Minnesota and northeast Iowa when they first met French traders and missionaries in the 1670s. At the time, the tribe enjoyed a fairly peaceful existence despite the presence of other tribes that sometimes made the upper Mississippi River valley a dangerous region. The Ioway were then chiefly allied with the Otoe and the Winnebago, who lived to the west of them. They also managed to maintain friendly relations with the Dakota, who lived to their northeast, and with the Dakota's enemies, the Sac and Fox, Illinois, and Potawatomi. The balance among the tribes was upset when the Iroquois nations and the French moved westward into what is now Wisconsin in the 1670s. The Ioways' ability to remain neutral during this period of instability may have come in part from their ability to form alliances and make peace with other tribes.

In 1676, one of the first French travelers to meet the Ioway, the Jesuit priest Louis André, commented that the tribe was "rich in buffalo hides and in red catlinite," the soft stone from which sacred pipes were made. The red stone came from quarries near

René Robert Cavelier, Sieur de la Salle, raised a cross and the French flag near the mouth of the Mississippi River in 1682, claiming the entire Mississippi River valley for France. (Courtesy of the State Historical Society of Missouri, Columbia.)

the present-day community of Pipestone in southwest Minnesota. André believed that the Ioway controlled access to the quarries and enjoyed power over other tribes as a result. While that may not have been true, it is certain that the Ioway introduced many of the tribes that they met on their travels to a solemn sacred pipe ceremony that created a bond of friendship and peace between them. This ceremony apparently often allowed the Ioway to travel unharmed through the territory of their neighbors.

As the Ioway worked to maintain political relations with neighboring Indian nations, they began to come into closer contact with the French traders and missionaries who moved into the upper Mississippi River valley from Canada. French missionaries introduced the Indians of the region to Christianity. Father André, for instance, reported that he took the opportunity to "preach Jesus Christ to them" during his first visit.

The French were also interested in developing trade relations with the Ioway, who first traveled to a French trading post, at the site of present-day Green Bay, Wisconsin, in the mid 1670s. It was not long before French traders sought out Ioway villages. One of the first to do so was Michel Accault. Accault spent long periods of time with the Ioway in 1678 and 1679, trading metal implements such as knives, awls, needles, axes, and kettles, as well as blankets, beads, and tobacco, for the hides of buffalo or beaver, which the Ioway called *thinye braxge,* or flat tails. As trade became more profitable, the French began to play a larger role in the everyday lives of the Ioway people.

In 1682, the French explorer René Robert Cavelier, Sieur de la Salle, traveled from the Great Lakes to the mouth of the Mississippi River and claimed its entire watershed for France, christening the region Louisiana in honor of King Louis XIV. Jacques de la Metarie, notary of the La Salle expedition, recorded the ceremony. Upon reaching the mouth of the Mississippi, the men prepared a cross and a column on which they attached the French seal. In a speech La Salle said that the Indian tribes in the area had assured him that the French were the first Europeans to travel down the river. He therefore claimed the land along the river and its tributaries, as well as its entire native population, for France. He then declared that his majesty would "annex no country to its crown without making it his chief care to establish the Christian religion therein," as the men hoisted the cross.

La Salle claimed the territory for France under the authority of a medieval European law known as the Doctrine of Discovery. European nations originally used the doctrine when they invaded Islamic portions of the Middle East during the Crusades of the eleventh and twelfth centuries. As Christians, these invaders believed they had a unique moral right to take possession of Islamic land in the name of the Catholic Church. When European nations later colonized the North and South American continents, this doctrine allowed them to claim Indian land and, in their view, gain absolute legal title to it. By using this doctrine, La Salle in effect made the Ioway and their neighbors subject to the French crown without their knowledge.

By the mid 1680s, French trade activity had increased under the direction of Nicholas Perrot, the commander of the trading fort at Green Bay. When he met with the Ioway in 1685, Perrot advised them that the demand for beaver pelts, which the Europeans used to make hats, was far greater than the need for bison hides and encouraged them to hunt and trap more beaver. Wanting French trade goods, the Ioway sent a hunting party to the headwaters of the Des Moines River in what is now southwest Minnesota and northwest Iowa in the winter of 1685–1686. With its abundance of backwaters, marshes, and lakes, the headwaters area was ideal for trapping beaver, and the effort seems to have been a success.

Beaver trapping marked the beginning of a significant change in the Ioways' lifestyle. As they became more deeply involved in the European trade economy, they gradually lost their self-sufficiency. By devoting increasing amounts of their time, energy, and resources to hunting for the purpose of trade, the Ioway had little time left to hunt for their own survival. When many of the tribe's hunters spent the winter of 1685–1686 trapping beaver, few were available for the Ioways' winter buffalo hunt. As a result, the smaller number of hunters did not always succeed in filling the Ioways' cache pits with enough dried meat to last through the year.

Increased dependence on trade had another effect on Ioway culture. Like many other Indian tribes, the Ioway developed a

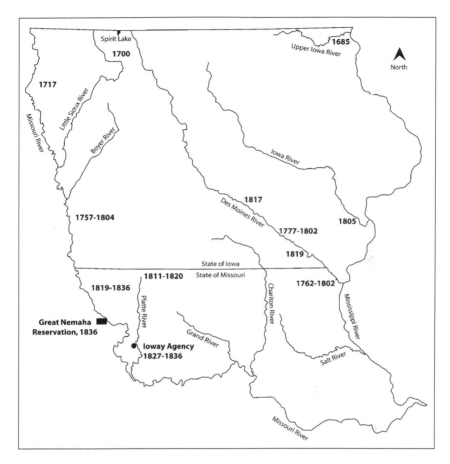

Map of Ioway settlements. This map shows that between 1685 and 1836, the Ioway Indians were highly mobile. During that time, they slowly migrated from the northern portion of the present-day state of Iowa to the northwest region of present-day Missouri. (Map by the author, based on Duane Anderson's "Iowa Ethnohistory," *Annals of Iowa*, vol. 41 [1971–1973].)

fondness for French trade goods made of metal. In fact, the Ioways' name for Europeans, *Ma'unke,* means makers of metal. Their increasing use of manufactured trade goods gradually drew them away from some of their cultural traditions. As the Ioway replaced their bone awls, ceramic kettles, and stone axes with more durable metal trade goods, the time-consuming process of making these traditional items for themselves gradually ended. The rituals connected with making utensils from the bones of animal relatives, from the grandfather rocks, and from the clay that was part of mother earth herself, had long reinforced the Ioways' concept of their place in the natural world. As they lost this knowledge and grew more dependent on others for their supplies, their relationship with the natural world began to change.

One of the most striking ways in which the friendship with the French changed the lives of the Ioway occurred on a far more personal level. As French traders traveled to Ioway villages, they began to develop close personal ties to members of the tribe. The French were known for their willingness to adapt to native ways of life while living on the frontier, and many traders married into Ioway families. These marriages seem natural given the long periods of time that many traders spent working and living with Ioway people. However, traders quickly discovered that marrying into the tribe was also good for business. Marriage to the daughter of a headman almost always assured a French trader of receiving favorable treatment in trade that could help improve his status as a businessman. The Ioway headman could also gain stature and authority within the tribe by forming a close, and sometimes exclusive, tie with French trade networks.

Sometimes, relations between traders and individual tribal members upset the traditional system of leadership within an Indian nation. By forming a close bond with a trader, a tribal member who did not have the status of a headman could gain control of a flow of trade goods, allowing him to gather and distribute wealth. Because a large part of a headman's status was related to his ability to provide for his people and give them what they needed, the wealth of these tribal members undercut the headmen's status. This created rivalries that eroded the unity of the tribe by causing jealousy and divisions within it.

The competition that came with the increase in trade activity also heightened tensions between native groups in the upper Mississippi River valley. In the 1680s, the Ioways' relationship with their Algonquin-speaking neighbors, the Illinois and the Mascoutin, began to sour as these tribes tried to control the Ioways' access to trade goods, especially firearms. After the Algonquians made an attack on one of their villages, the Ioway left the region. They moved west to the vicinity of Spirit Lake in present-day northwest Iowa to be closer to their source of valuable beaver pelts and to their allies the Otoe and the Omaha. Still, warfare continued to keep them on the move. Fighting between the Dakota and their relatives from the Great Plains, the Lakota, eventually forced the Ioway down the Missouri River to live near the site of present-day Omaha, Nebraska. It was here, archaeologists believe, that the Ioway came into contact with other Plains tribes who introduced them to yet another influence which would change their lives forever: the horse.

After 1700, the possibility of profits to be made in lead mining and the fur trade lured French explorers and traders from New Orleans to the mouth of the Missouri River. They were not alone, however, in their interest in the region they called Louisiana and feared that their colonial rivals, the Spanish and the English, would challenge them for its resources. From their colonial capital in Santa Fe, Spain controlled a sizable amount of territory southwest of Louisiana. Meanwhile, the British were firmly entrenched on the eastern seaboard. To protect their land in the Mississippi Valley and to develop trade relations with the natives, the French constructed a number of forts along the Mississippi and Missouri Rivers beginning in 1719. The first French post on the Missouri River was Fort Orleans, built on the river's north bank near the mouth of the Grand River in 1723 under the command of Etienne de Véniard, Sieur de Bourgmont.

Bourgmont was the first white man known to have explored the lower Missouri River valley. From 1712 to 1719 he had lived close to a Missouria village near the present-day site of

Brunswick, Missouri, undertaking expeditions upriver. He married a Missouria woman and, when he returned to France in 1720, took their six-year-old son, called Petit Missouri, with him. By 1723, Bourgmont was back along the Missouri River, where he returned his son to his Missouria family and carried out his orders to establish Fort Orleans. The French planned to use the fort as a base to establish and protect trade networks with tribes in the area. Bourgmont asked members of the Missouria and the Osage to help lead his men on an expedition upriver to establish peaceful trade relations with tribes such as the Otoe and the Kansas. This trip also provided him with a chance to establish friendly relations with the Ioway when he met with six of the tribe's headmen on October 5, 1724, in a Kansas village near the Kansas River.

Because of the enormous size of Louisiana and the fact that it was located far from the centers of the French colonial government in Canada and New Orleans, the post proved expensive to maintain and defend, and was abandoned after Bourgmont returned to France. The Company of the Indies kept a garrison there for a time, but despite Bourgmont's apparent success at establishing relations with the region's native people during his stay there, the company abandoned the fort in 1728.

Anticipated profits from the Louisiana territory never materialized, and the Seven Years' War with Britain, known as the French and Indian War in the American colonies, was a serious strain on the French treasury. Realizing that they were in a conflict they could not win, France ceded the territory of Louisiana to its ally Spain in the secretly negotiated Treaty of Fontaine-bleau in 1762. The following year the war ended, with France surrendering Canada and all of its territory east of the Mississippi to Britain in the Treaty of Paris.

During Louisiana's slow transition from French to Spanish rule, the Ioway left the Missouri River, where their onetime allies the Omaha, Otoe, and Dakota had begun to challenge them over hunting land, and made their way to the Des Moines River in what is now southeast Iowa. In an effort to ensure that

Engraving of Sac and Fox by Karl Bodmer. Originating east of the Great Lakes—some say as far east as the Atlantic coast—the Algonquin-speaking Sac and Fox Indians were so closely allied that some considered them to be a single tribe. After they first entered Ioway land west of the Missouri River in the middle of the eighteenth century, relations between the Ioway and the Sac and Fox were often cooperative, but sometimes violent. (Courtesy of the State Historical Society of Missouri, Columbia.)

they would retain their access to trade in their new location, the Ioway sent a party to meet with the French trader Pierre Laclede, who had founded the new settlement of St. Louis in 1764. Under the terms of an agreement they reached with Laclede, two French traders traveled to the Des Moines River for the sole purpose of doing business with the Ioway.

As the Spanish moved into St. Louis and the British established themselves east of the Mississippi, native tribes in the region often were caught in the middle as the two European nations competed for power and trade. At times, the Spanish and British both used intertribal conflicts to their own advan-

Indian Attack on the Village of St. Louis, 1780, by Oscar E. Berninghous. Throughout much of the end of the eighteenth century and the beginning of the nineteenth century, some Ioway were closely allied with the British. In 1776 seven Ioway headmen and their families traveled to Montreal with a delegation of Dakota, Winnebago, and Sac and Fox to forge an alliance with Frederick Haldimand, governor and chief of the British provinces. Two years later Ioway warriors joined the British in an unsuccessful attack on St. Louis. (Lunette mural from the Missouri State Capitol, reproduction courtesy of the State Historical Society of Missouri, Columbia.)

tage. The Osage, often at odds with the Spanish, bore the brunt of several attacks from their many Indian rivals—the Ioway and the Sac and Fox among them. On more than one occasion, the Spanish were instrumental in provoking these attacks.

At the same time, the Ioway took advantage of the unstable political situation in upper Louisiana. From their villages they had easy access both to Spanish trade goods coming from St. Louis and British goods from a post at Prairie du Chien in present-day Wisconsin. While they generally preferred the higher quality of both the merchandise and the trade relations offered by the English, the Ioway were more than willing to conduct business with the Spanish in Louisiana when it was in their best interests.

While the Ioways' move back to the Des Moines River brought them closer to both British and Spanish trade goods, it also brought them into contact with two Algonquin-speaking tribes that would have a great influence over Ioway life for decades to come. The Sac and the Fox first crossed the Mississippi River into Ioway lands in the middle of the eighteenth century in search of safety. The tribes, which had their origins in what is now the eastern United States, had most recently lived in the central Great Lakes region until forced to move because of warfare with the French. They eventually returned to the east side of the Mississippi River to settle along the Rock River in what is now northern Illinois. However, as the growing population of settlers in the Illinois country strained the area's natural resources, the Sac and Fox sometimes cautiously traveled back into Ioway territory to hunt. In return for being allowed to use Ioway hunting land west of the river, the Sac and Fox helped the Ioway defend the western and southern borders of their land. This alliance with the Sac and Fox, as well as their access to British firearms, enabled the Ioway to retain control of most of present-day Iowa and to push into the lower Missouri River valley, challenging the Osage, Kansas, Missouria, and Otoe for domination of that land.

The Ioways' efforts to maintain control over their territory also affected their relations with the British and the Spanish. By the end of the 1770s the Ioways' relationship with the Spanish was becoming increasingly hostile as their alliance with the British, who had established themselves in Canada, became stronger. In 1776 seven Ioway headmen and their families had traveled to Montreal with a delegation of Dakota, Winnebago, and Sac and Fox to meet with Frederick Haldimand, governor and chief of the British provinces. On behalf of King George III, Haldimand awarded some of the more prominent headmen, including an Ioway whose name was recorded as Le Voleur, or The Thief, with medals of friendship and peace. The inscription on Le Voleur's medal signified the British crown's optimistic hope of a prolonged relationship with the Ioway as the American War for Independence intensified:

> In consideration of loyalty, attachment shown by Le Voleur, great chief of the Zaivovois [Ioways], to His Majesty's Government, and by means of my authority and power, I confirm by this great medal, that I wish that all Indians living at his place obey him as the great chief, and that he be considered as such by His Majesty's all others subjects.

Four years later, on May 26, 1780, Ioway and Sac and Fox fighting men joined warriors from other tribes to help their British trading allies in an attack on St. Louis. The 650 Indian warriors who raided the settlement far outnumbered the 350 Spanish militia men, led by Captain Fernando de Leyba, who defended it. The Indians, however, were not able to overcome the power of the militia's cannons, and the land west of the Mississippi River remained under Spanish control. Though the Indians did not succeed in destroying the settlement of 700, they reportedly killed 18, wounded 6, and captured 57. The end of the American Revolution in December 1783 forced the Ioway and Sac and Fox to travel to Canada to maintain their trading relationship with the British traders. This prompted the Spanish-sponsored traders in upper Louisiana to complain that the British were cutting into their business and stirring the Indians to acts of violence against Spanish subjects.

By the early 1800s, the Ioway occupied a large and important geographical region. They claimed to control much of the land that makes up the present-day state of Iowa and the northern part of present-day Missouri. This region was roughly defined by the border between Iowa and Minnesota on the north and the Little Sioux and Missouri Rivers on the west. The southern portion of the Ioways' territory extended along the Missouri River to the Grand River in present-day Missouri. It may have also included the land between the Chariton River and the Mississippi River, as far south as the Salt River, in what are now Ralls and Monroe Counties in Missouri. Though the Otoe-Missouria, Kansas, Osage, Omaha, Yankton Dakota, and Sac and Fox all contested the Ioways' claim to this land, for a time the Ioway occupied significant portions of the area.

The Ioways' control of the region would not last, however. As early as the 1780s a more assertive group of immigrants had already begun to arrive in the Mississippi River valley. After the American colonies gained independence from Britain in 1783, a "white tide" of American settlers rapidly spread from the East Coast to the Mississippi River. The arrival of the Americans would lead to even more rapid and significant changes in the Ioway people's way of life.

3

A Troubled Time between the
Ioway and the United States

The Ioway had met in council for the first time with a representative of the American colonies, soon to become the United States, in 1778. The meeting was led by a brash young lieutenant colonel of the Continental Army named George Rogers Clark. In the summer of that year Clark led a small force of about 175 men into the town of Kaskaskia, in the Illinois country, along the Mississippi River, hoping to gain the support of the old French "habitants" of what was then British soil. After he successfully convinced the habitants to ally themselves with the colonies in their war for independence from Britain, Clark hoped to do the same with the region's Indian population.

In August 1778 Clark sent messages to the tribes, summoning them to a council at the site of the ancient city of Cahokia. The Ioway attended, as did their Siouan relatives the Winnebago, their enemies the Osage, and their allies the Sac and Fox. Clark addressed the delegates, warning them that if they failed to support the colonies in their war with Britain, they would suffer the wrath of the American military. Because Clark's colonial forces were still small in number, however, his threats failed to convince the Ioway to drop their allegiance to the British.

After the United States gained independence from Britain, however, the number of Americans making their way to the Mississippi River began to increase. West of the river, Spanish officials in upper Louisiana watched the growing American population closely. Like the French before them, the Spanish found the large territory of Louisiana difficult to govern. Spain never succeeded in allotting enough resources to the territory either to manage relations with the native tribes or to control the threat posed by the British traders. Hoping to remedy this situation, the Spanish extended an offer of free land grants to American settlers who were willing to cross the Mississippi River to live in the territory as Spanish subjects. Between 1796 and 1800, hundreds of settlers accepted land grants and moved onto plots that were mostly located along the Mississippi and Missouri Rivers. One of the most famous of these settlers was the frontiersman Daniel Boone, who received a thousand arpents, or about 850 acres, of land near present-day Marthasville, Missouri, and settled there with his family and friends in 1799.

But even this influx of new citizens did not provide the Spanish government with the level of control that it desired. In 1800, Spain returned Louisiana to France, and France sold it to the United States in 1803. Meanwhile, settlers continued to flood into the region in such numbers that by the time the U.S. flag was raised over St. Louis in March 1804, there were as many American and European immigrants in upper Louisiana as there were Indians.

As the population of upper Louisiana increased, competition for land, wild game, and other natural resources became more intense. Like most tribes in the region, the estimated eight hundred Ioway people living in what is now Missouri grew more dependent than ever on the goods they acquired by trading furs. The trader Pierre Chouteau, whose trading post was located near the Osage villages, but who also traded with several other tribes in the region, estimated that the Ioway had traded for $12,000— or the present-day equivalent of $150,000—worth of goods annually in 1803 and 1804. Thus, they counted on the local animal population not only for their own needs but also to secure furs for trade. Since they had begun trading with the French more than a century earlier, native hunters in the Mississippi and Missouri River basins had harvested increasingly large numbers of animal pelts each year. In the 1750s, for example, a French official estimated that the Ioway and Otoe were trading 80 packs of animal skins per year. By 1805, the explorer Zebulon Pike estimated that the Ioway alone traded 300 packs of animal hides per year and the Sac and Fox traded 1,000 packs annually. A pack was a standard-sized bundle of furs commonly used in trading. Each pack contained approximately 50 fox skins, 60 beaver pelts, or 10 buffalo robes. In order to maintain this volume of trade, all of the tribes in the region jealously guarded whatever hunting lands they were able to defend from the growing number of native and American competitors moving into the area.

The increasing competition soon strained the long-standing alliance between the Ioway and the Sac and Fox. The Ioway came to resent the frequent hunting trips their allies made in the vicinity of Ioway villages west of the Mississippi River. By 1807, their rivalry over land turned violent when the Sac and Fox under the leadership of Black Hawk began to lead raids on Ioway villages. The Ioway retaliated, and episodes of warfare between the once-friendly tribes began.

As the game near their villages became depleted, the Ioway traveled west to the lower Missouri River in search of buffalo. These hunting trips proved to be dangerous because they brought the Ioway into contact—and sometimes into violent conflict—with the Osage and Kansas, who felt that the Ioway presence in the Missouri River country violated their own hunting rights to that land. This competition for hunting rights touched off decades of bloody warfare between the Ioway and Osage.

※　※　※

The westward expansion of the United States signaled great changes in the lives of the Ioway and their neighboring tribes. In the beginning, the American government was as poorly prepared to govern the huge territory as the French and Spanish had been. The $15 million they had spent to acquire the territory put a huge strain on the federal treasury and there was, as yet, no significant U.S. government or military presence inside the territory for protection of its citizens.

Despite the fact that the Ioway and several other Indian nations still claimed upper Louisiana as their own, the federal government encouraged settlers to move west of the Mississippi to begin developing and securing the territory. Rumors reached St. Louis in September 1804 that the Ioway, Potawatomi, and Sac and Fox had joined to protect the land south of their Des Moines River villages from white settlers. When settlers found two white men murdered near the Cuivre River northwest of St. Louis that same month, they blamed the tribal alliance. Afraid more attacks would follow, settlers left their farms and banded together for protection, appealing to James Wilkinson, the first U.S.-appointed governor of upper Louisiana, for support in the form of arms or militia troops.

Wilkinson's concerns about this violence were twofold. First, he feared that conflict with the tribal alliance would become more frequent as white settlement increased. He was also concerned that British traders from Wisconsin with whom the Ioway and Sac and Fox regularly did business would encourage them to commit more violent acts to weaken U.S. control over the territory. In order to prevent this, he made an effort to strengthen the tiny armed militia the territorial government had established in St. Louis in 1804. The task of gaining an upper hand in Louisiana, however, was overwhelming. As Wilkinson wrote to Secretary of War Henry Dearborn in September 1805, "When I cast my eyes over the expanse of Territory to be occupied or controlled . . . [I observe] that we are not of sufficient strength of men or means to meet the occasion."

❈   ❈   ❈

Even before the Louisiana Purchase was complete, Thomas Jefferson had planned a "Corps of Discovery" to travel up the Missouri River to search for a water route to the Pacific Ocean and to get a better sense of the size and character of the vast territory west of the Mississippi River. In May of 1804 Captains Meriwether Lewis and William Clark, younger brother of George Rogers Clark, departed from St. Charles with approximately thirty-five soldiers and a dozen hired French boatmen on a two-year journey that was part military expedition, part political mission, and part scientific scouting party.

The corps was the first U.S. attempt at diplomacy with the Indian people who lived west of the Mississippi River. Lewis and Clark prepared for the mission by taking gifts, medals, and a message to present to each of the tribes they encountered on their travels. At the beginning of their journey, however, they had a difficult time locating any Indian people. Many of the tribes who normally lived along the river were camping in the western prairies on their summer buffalo hunts. As the members of the Corps of Discovery passed through the lower Missouri River, they found only uninhabited village sites. It was not until August 3, 1804, when they were just north of the site of present-day Omaha, Nebraska, that they had their first chance to meet face-to-face with an Indian delegation. On a high hill overlooking the Missouri River which from that day on would be known as Council Bluff, a small group of Otoe-Missouria men led by Little Thief and Big Horse accepted Lewis and Clark's invitation to meet with them. Lewis and Clark presented the Otoe-Missouria with gifts and certificates that declared them to be friends and allies of the United States.

While Lewis and Clark saw their journey as a chance to make friends with the native population that lived along the Missouri River, some tribes apparently believed the expedition was an invitation to meet directly with government officials in Washington. Even though Lewis and Clark did not meet directly with members of the Ioway tribe as they traveled up the Missouri River, a group of Ioway headmen arrived in St. Louis

in November 1804 and reported that Captain Lewis had promised them a trip to the U.S. capital city. Other Indian groups
appeared soon after with the same story. Pierre Chouteau, the
Osages' Indian agent, who also traded regularly with the Ioway
and several other local tribes, asked President Thomas Jefferson
for permission to send the Indian delegates on to Washington.
Both Chouteau and the Indians were soon disappointed, however, as neither Jefferson nor his secretary of war, Henry
Dearborn, granted permission for them to travel beyond St.
Louis at that time.

An important part of the Corps of Discovery's mission was to
inform the tribes along the Missouri River that they were no
longer under French or Spanish rule. The expedition's leaders
wanted the Indian nations to know that the president of the
United States, Thomas Jefferson, was now their "Great Father."
They stressed that Jefferson was a benevolent leader who
wished to befriend them, treat them fairly, and to "aid them in
all the improvements which may better their condition."

In fact, what Jefferson had in mind for his Indian "children"
who lived west of the Mississippi River was to use their land to
resettle Indian tribes from east of the river to make room for
white settlers moving west. Jefferson reasoned that by placing
the great river between the natives and settlers, he could avoid
the violence he feared increasing settlement would cause.

Just a few months after the Corps of Discovery began its journey, the U.S. government made its first attempt to buy clear title
to Indian land west of the Mississippi River. In the fall of 1804,
General William Henry Harrison met with five low-level Sac
and Fox headmen in St. Louis. While the two tribes were not
alone in using violent methods to protect their homeland, they
had gained a reputation for being especially hostile toward the
Americans. Harrison proposed that the Sac and Fox sell their
claim to a huge portion of land that stretched along the
Mississippi River from St. Louis north into present-day
Wisconsin. Despite the fact that they lacked tribal authority to
do so, the five Sac and Fox representatives agreed to sell the

land for $2,234.50 plus $1,000 in annuities. After learning of the treaty, Black Hawk and other higher-ranking leaders of the Sac and Fox protested the agreement, resulting in a struggle that lasted for decades.

This treaty revealed a policy that did not bode well for the Ioway and their Indian neighbors. It showed that the Americans viewed native claims to land in ways that distinguished them from their predecessors. The colonial governments of France, Spain, and Britain had been content to share the land with native people. The American government, however, quickly set about pressuring the tribes to give up their claims to the land that the U.S. Congress officially christened the Territory of Louisiana in 1805.

In October 1805 it was the Ioways' turn to meet in a treaty council with officials of the United States. Governor Wilkinson and General Harrison summoned the Ioway and members of nine other tribes, including the Osage and the Sac and Fox, to St. Louis for a council to try to bring an end to their recent acts of violence against settlers. Harrison and Wilkinson proposed that the tribes agree to two treaty articles. First, they asked the tribes to pledge their loyalty to the United States and to promise to end all violent acts against U.S. citizens and members of other native nations. Second, they asked the tribes to bring any disagreements that might arise between them to the territorial government to be settled peacefully. Twelve headmen, including an Ioway headman the Americans called Voi Ri Gran, agreed to the treaty document.

As was the case with many peace councils held at the time, the goodwill and friendship expressed in St. Louis was short-lived. This was primarily because peace agreements like the Treaty of 1805 did nothing to help native people solve the problems that led to violence in the first place. The Indian nations along the Mississippi were suffering as greater numbers of both native and nonnative people moved into their homelands. Competition for wild game and other natural resources became fierce, and many tribes found it difficult to maintain the standard of living they had once enjoyed. Furthermore, neither the federal nor territorial governments had enough military strength to prevent tribes from moving onto one another's land to hunt. Troops were also unable to keep American settlers from squatting in areas still held by native landowners. When violence did erupt, the limited military forces were unable to bring justice to the frontier in a way that satisfied either the settlers or the natives. As a result, victims on both sides regularly chose to seek their own revenge rather than to rely on slow-moving territorial justice.

Just days after the conclusion of the treaty council in St. Louis, twenty-six representatives from eleven Indian nations, including the Osage, Sac and Fox, and Ioway tribes, embarked on a trip to Washington to meet with President Jefferson. This meeting not only presented the Ioway with their first opportunity to meet their Great Father but also gave Jefferson a chance to stress, once again, the basic points of his government's Indian policy. When Jefferson spoke to his Indian guests in January 1806, he reminded them that the United States had forced the Spanish, French, and British from the Louisiana Territory forever and was in the region to stay. He warned the tribes that the Americans were as "numerous as the stars in the heavens . . . and [were] all strong men." He advised them to learn to live peacefully with one another and with their new American neighbors. To help them accomplish this, the president promised to assign a "Father," or Indian agent, to live among them. Any disagreements that arose between them were not to be settled in bloodshed, he told them, but were to be taken to their Father for peaceful settlement.

Upon their return home, the Ioway learned that Nicolas Boilvin, a French Canadian and a former employee of trader August Chouteau, would be their new "Father." Secretary of War Henry Dearborn assigned Boilvin to live in a Sac and Fox village located on the Mississippi near the mouth of the Des Moines River and instructed him to interact regularly with all of the Ioway and Sac and Fox in the region.

As agent, it was Boilvin's job to see that two important elements of American Indian policy were applied to the three tribes under his watch. He was first to ensure that the Ioway and the Sac and Fox remain friendly to the United States and that they end their acts of violence. Dearborn further ordered the new agent to "teach the Indians such of the arts of agriculture and domestic manufactures, as your situation will allow." The War Department hired a farmer to instruct the Indians in the latest European-American methods of agriculture and Dearborn promised to send a blacksmith to the Sac and Fox village as soon as possible.

About fourteen hundred Ioway were living in two main villages, one on the Des Moines River and one on the Iowa River, when Boilvin went to live with them in 1805. The Ioway population had been diminished by a serious smallpox epidemic in 1803 that by some estimates killed as many as one hundred men and an untold number of women and children. When explorer Zebulon Montgomery Pike traveled up the Mississippi River that summer, he observed that the Ioway were somewhat "backward," noting that because they did not live directly on the Mississippi with the Sac and Fox, they were "less civilized than those nations." Though he judged them to be "out of the high road of commerce," Pike reported that the Ioway regularly traded black bear, beaver, otter, mink, gray fox, muskrat, and deer skins with British traders from Mackinac.

The U.S government's worries that these British contacts were leading the Ioway and Sac and Fox to acts of violence against American settlers seemed justified after two high-profile murders involving tribal members occurred. In 1807, a Sac and Fox man named Little Crow killed a trader named Antoine Le Page near St. Louis at Portage de Sioux. A year later, two Ioway men, White Cloud and another identified as Mera Nautais, were charged with the deaths of two traders on the Missouri River near the site of present-day Brunswick, Missouri. The incident involving the two Ioway men occurred while they were returning

John B. C. Lucas moved to St. Louis in September 1805 after President Thomas Jefferson appointed him to be a justice in the Louisiana Territory's supreme court and a member of the territory's board of land commissioners. In August 1808, Lucas presided over the trial of two Ioway men, MaxúThka (White Cloud) and Mera Nautais, who were charged with killing two French traders on the Missouri River. Though the jury convicted both men, Lucas prevented the sentence of death from being carried out because he believed the crime had occurred outside the court's jurisdiction. (Courtesy of the State Historical Society of Missouri, Columbia.)

from a raid on the Osage. As they stood on shore waiting to cross the river, four French traders who were traveling in a canoe opened fire on them. In the firefight that followed, two of the traders, Joseph Merachal and Joseph Tebeau, died.

News of these events increased already tense relations between Indians and U.S. settlers in the Territory of Louisiana. While the tribes wanted to atone for the murders in the traditional way, by repaying the victims' families with horses and other goods, Meriwether Lewis, who had been named territorial governor in 1808, believed he should make a show by severely punishing those responsible for the murders. With the help of twenty-seven infantrymen and a six-hundred-dollar reward, agent Boilvin was able to convince the Sac and Fox and the Ioway to deliver the accused men to St. Louis for trial.

The Ioway defendants were tried and convicted in St. Louis in July 1808. While the jury sentenced them to death for the killings, Judge John B. C. Lucas granted White Cloud and Mera Nautais a new trial in order to reexamine the court's authority in the matter. Lucas ruled that the territorial court could not punish the Ioway because the crime occurred on land that had not been ceded to the United States. Concerned about the public outcry that was sure to erupt if the two convicted Indian murderers were released, Governor Lewis ordered that they remain in jail while the case awaited further review. The situation remained unsettled until the two escaped from jail the following year.

Meanwhile, in a separate trial Little Crow was also sentenced to death for Le Page's murder. Because he had committed the crime inside the boundaries of the land ceded to the United States in the Treaty of 1804, the court ruled that it did have the right to uphold his sentence. However, President Jefferson feared Indian revenge and was unwilling to allow Little Crow's execution. Like White Cloud and Mera Nautais, Little Crow remained in jail for more than a year. After the two Ioway escaped, William Clark, acting as the U.S. Indian agent in St. Louis, recommended that Little Crow be pardoned. Newly elected President James Madison signed the pardon in the hope that the Sac and Fox would "behave well in the future."

However, violence in Louisiana did not end. Nor did the Americans succeed in persuading the Ioway and the Sac and Fox to end their political and economic ties with the British. In fact, over the coming years, that relationship would only become stronger. This proved to be a major frustration for the Americans, whose own ties with the British were rapidly deteriorating. Some feared that war between the two nations was inevitable. The Americans worried that if war did break out, Britain's Indian allies would bring the fighting to the Louisiana Territory. As it turned out, these fears proved well founded.

4

War in the Ioway Homeland

During the first decade of the nineteenth century the world in which the Ioway lived was marked by an expanded U.S. military presence and more bloodshed. The growing population of settlers and more competition for hunting grounds led to increasing hostility among native people in the Louisiana Territory. The federal government's relations with some tribes, most notably the Osage, grew more hostile and intertribal warfare was also on the rise. As relations with the Osage worsened, Territorial Governor Meriwether Lewis encouraged some of their long-standing enemies to band together to force the Osage out of the territory. The Ioway eagerly took part in the U.S. campaign, as did the Shawnee, a tribe from the eastern United States forced to make a new home in Louisiana on the eastern edge of Osage territory.

Closer to the Ioway villages, the Ioway and Sac and Fox were once again at war. White settlement in Wisconsin and Illinois forced the Sac and Fox to rely more heavily on Ioway land east of the Mississippi River for hunting. The Ioways' attempts to keep their territory led to attacks against them in return. In the winter of 1808 agent Nicolas Boilvin reported that Sac and Fox men had killed several Ioway. Governor Lewis threatened to punish the tribes with trade sanctions but decided against the idea, perhaps out of fear that it would cause them to strengthen their already friendly relations with the British. Instead he enlisted the help of the trader Denis Julien, whose wife, Catherine, was Ioway, in an effort to mend relations between the Ioway and the United States by offering the tribe greater access to U.S. goods.

If ongoing intertribal warfare worried the United States, rumors of an Indian war confederacy was cause for even greater alarm. In 1808 several Ioway men joined members of the Sac and Fox, Menominee, and Winnebago on a trip to the Wabash River in present-day Indiana to visit the Shawnee prophet Tenskwatawa. Tenskwatawa and his brother Tecumseh were traveling throughout the Ohio and Mississippi River valleys to speak with various tribes in an attempt to unite native people. Tenskwatawa told of a vision he had in which native people returned to prosperity by embracing their traditional ways and rejecting the ways of the white people. The brothers believed that only by forgetting their own differences and joining together in a military alliance with the British could native people drive out their common enemy, the United States.

Perhaps because they lived under the watchful eye of their "American father" Boilvin, or maybe because they could not overcome their long-running dispute with some of their native neighbors, the Ioway did not join the confederacy, and Tenskwatawa and Tecumseh ultimately failed to enlist the number of fighting men needed to become a serious threat to westward expansion.

The Ioway did, however, join the Osage and Sac and Fox in harassing the traders and settlers who began to move into the lower Missouri River valley. In response to unrest among the Indian tribes in the Louisiana Territory, the United States established two important military posts that directly affected the

Ioway people. In 1808 Fort Osage was built in present-day Jackson County on a high bluff overlooking the Missouri River. William Clark had noted the site four years earlier on the Corps of Discovery expedition. At the time it was built, Fort Osage was the American military's most westerly outpost. Clark thought the location of the fort, which was part trading post, or "factory," and part military stockade, was ideal because it was less than sixty miles from the villages of the Osage and the hunting grounds of several other tribes including the Ioway, Kansas, and Sac and Fox. Governor Lewis hoped the presence of American traders and soldiers would ease tensions in the region. In July he optimistically predicted that "by compelling several nations to trade at the same establishment, they will find it absolutely necessary to live in peace with each other."

In an attempt to repair the U.S. government's rocky relations with the Osage, Clark called several members of the tribe to the site of the new fort in November 1808. During the council Clark convinced the Osage that the American post was in their best interests because it would provide them with access to trade goods and military protection, and he asked the tribe to cede a large portion of tribal land in what is now western Missouri and northwestern Arkansas to the United States. After a year of negotiations, the Osage finally agreed to the treaty in August of 1809, and their hostility toward the United States officially ceased.

The U.S. military established a second fort on the Mississippi River that was practically within view of the Ioway and Sac and Fox villages. As had been the case with Fort Osage, the Americans hoped that their presence at Fort Madison, located at the site of the Iowa town that bears its name today, would discourage the three tribes from continuing their acts of violence. Military officials believed that the location of the fort on the Mississippi would also allow them to monitor and disrupt the flow of British trade goods to Indians living in American territory. However, the Sac and Fox and Ioway proved less interested than the Osage in cooperating with American military officials. The Sac and Fox were hostile toward the soldiers, and one group of warriors led by Black Hawk unsuccessfully attempted to trick the Americans into letting them enter the fort so that they could attack the soldiers living inside. In response, Governor Lewis ordered 140 additional troops to march north from St. Louis immediately to help secure the post.

As the United States continued to have troubled relations with the British and the native people on the upper Mississippi River, President Thomas Jefferson realized that an Indian ally was desperately needed in the region. In 1809 he attempted to create such an ally by boldly trying to influence the political leadership of the Ioway nation. That summer, Jefferson authorized Hard Heart to receive documents and a medal naming him head chief of all the Ioway people.

In the eyes of government officials this title gave Hard Heart sole authority to negotiate treaties with the United States on behalf of the Ioway. Such actions were a common part of the American government's Indian policy, and French, Spanish, and British colonial officials had used similar tactics when dealing with Indian tribes. Traders and government officials who tried to negotiate with the Ioway and other Indian nations in Louisiana had long found it difficult to reach agreements with tribes. Making treaties in councils with many clan leaders and headmen not only tried the patience of territorial officials but also sometimes led to unpredictable results. By the second half of the eighteenth century the Spanish, French, and British had all discovered that it was quicker and easier to bypass the traditional channels of tribal leadership and forge alliances with specific individuals who could be relied upon to support colonial goals.

In this way, government powers essentially "created" tribal chiefs. They made these chiefs powerful among their own people by showering them with gifts and allowing them privileged access to trade goods. Engraved peace medals were especially popular gifts with Indian leaders. Much like the bear claw necklaces traditionally worn by Ioway headmen as emblems of their spiritual and social leadership status within the tribe, the highly prized European and American peace medals became powerful symbols that lent their owners an air of authority. However, the Americans' efforts to win the friendship of the Ioway with peace medals did not always succeed. James Wilkinson reported that during the Ioways' 1806 visit to Washington, one of the tribe's headmen returned a small U.S. peace medal because he preferred the larger medal the British had given him earlier.

Direct access to the flow of trade goods also gave these appointed "chiefs" the power to control the way in which goods were distributed among tribal members. Leaders favored by European and American colonial officials often had a powerful advantage over other leaders in the tribe. Colonial officials thus upset the balance of tribal politics by selecting a man who did not have traditional headman status within a tribe and making him the tribe's "chief." While this was sometimes the result of the officials' sheer ignorance of tribal politics, it was just as often part of a deliberate attempt to influence a tribe's political loyalties.

The presidential medal and papers awarded to Hard Heart gave him a level of authority that was unknown to traditional Ioway leaders. The idea that one individual might make decisions for the entire tribe went against the desire for the balance of powers that was one of the hallmarks of Ioway culture. Even though Hard Heart rightfully held the hereditary title of headman among the Ioway, his new privileged status with the U.S. government raised concerns both within and outside the tribe.

In September 1809 Frederick Bates, acting as territorial governor of the Louisiana Territory in the absence of Meriwether Lewis, worried that President Jefferson's recognition of Hard Heart had been a mistake. "Hard Heart has acted with too much hate and passion," wrote Bates, "and I believe him to be a man of native viciousness of temper." With a note of resignation, however, Bates added, "This man Hard Heart was made a Chief by the President himself, and I doubt our power to degrade him." Bates apparently believed that demotion could only come at the hands of members of Hard Heart's own tribe. "Our emblems of distinction might indeed be conferred on others but it is my first impression that a deprivation of Honors already bestowed is an Act exclusively of his own People." In other words, it was within Jefferson's power to create an Ioway chief, but it was up to the tribe to take that power away.

Despite Hard Heart's alleged fierce temper, Jefferson had formed a friendship with him because he led a segment of the Ioway that supported the U.S. government in its disagreements with the British. The Americans hoped that Hard Heart would be able to convince all of the Ioway to support the United States. But as war with Great Britain approached, the Ioway remained divided in their loyalties. The location of their Des Moines and Iowa River villages had long allowed them to enjoy the benefits of relations and trade with both the Americans and the British. Experience had taught them not to rely on a single foreign power. In the previous 125 years, they had seen both the French and the Spanish move onto Ioway land, only to be forced out by other nations. To side with one superpower in a time of war meant subjecting themselves to the certain wrath of the other, so most Ioway may not have been eager to ally themselves solely with either the Americans or the British.

While the threat of war in the northern portion of their homeland occupied the Ioway, their ongoing conflict with the Osage forced them to focus on their land to the south along the Missouri River as well. On December 5, 1810, George Sibley, the factor at Fort Osage, reported that two hundred Ioway and Sac warriors had attacked a party of Osage men and women who had been hunting along the Lamine River two days earlier. The war party "killed and took prisoner 5 men and 1 boy of the [Osage] party, and plundered them of several horses and all of their Peltry provisions, etc."

By 1811 clashes between the Osage and the Ioway were becoming increasingly bloody. The Osage complained to Sibley about the Ioways' violent attacks, threatening to resort to the "tomahawk and the scalping knife" if the U.S. government did not step in to punish them. In March, soldiers at the fort began to assist Osage war parties by ferrying them across the Missouri River as they made their way north to Ioway villages.

That same month, as the English botanist John Bradbury traveled up the Missouri River with an American Fur Company expedition, he heard rumors that three hundred Ioway, Potawatomi, Dakota, and Sac and Fox men were moving toward Fort Osage to attack the Osage nation. Days later he reported that the Ioway were soundly defeated in the battle and lost at least seven of their men.

On May 5, 1811, Sibley reported that the Osage had chopped into "50 pieces" an Ioway spy they had discovered just three hundred yards from Fort Osage. Two days later he described in grisly detail the celebrations of Osage victors after another unsuccessful Ioway raid the previous night. One Osage leader known as Sans Oreille was so eager to share the news of the Ioway defeat that he barged into Sibley's sleeping quarters in the middle of the night with a burning torch in one hand and the severed head of a slain Ioway "spy" in the other. Sibley quickly dressed and ran to the nearby Osage village, where he found them "in a temper far more Savage than I had ever before believed them capable," describing how the Osage proudly displayed for him a leg, finger, foot, and strips of skin from the body of "a distinguished Ioway war Chief."

Stories of acts like this spread fear and panic throughout Louisiana's growing population of Americans. Backcountry settlers, many squatting on land still rightfully claimed by the Ioway, worried that they were at risk of an Indian attack. Although a large part of the Louisiana Territory officially became the Territory of Missouri on June 4, 1812, fears increased when President James Madison signed the declaration of war against Britain two weeks later, on June 18. With less than 250 regular army troops stationed in the entire territory at that time, settlers quickly realized they had to rely on themselves for protection.

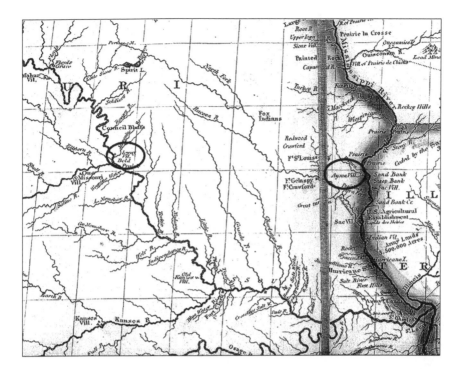

After the War of 1812, the Ioway were scattered between the Missouri and Mississippi Rivers. This detailed view of a map of the United States made by John Melish in 1816 shows two large Ioway villages separated by more than 250 miles. The eastern village is located on the Iowa River in present-day southeast Iowa. The western village is shown near the location of the present-day city of Council Bluffs, Iowa. Some historians believe a political rift among members of the Ioway tribe caused this division while others believe that a portion of the tribe moved west simply because there was not enough game to support the entire nation near the Iowa River village. (Courtesy of the Missouri State Archives.)

In the fast-growing Boonslick region about 140 miles west of St. Louis, settlers banded together to construct stockades in which as many as twenty families lived. Elsewhere, citizens formed companies of rangers to patrol the frontier, build fortifications, and gather intelligence about the movements of the British and their Indian allies. These rangers provided their own food, clothing, weapons, and horses for which the government did not reimburse them until after the War of 1812 ended.

By the time the war began, the Ioway had already been engaged in a prolonged struggle to protect their land, and some were battle-weary. Others, however, welcomed the war because they saw it as a chance to join forces with the British to drive the Americans from their land once and for all. Despite Hard Heart's support of the United States, most Ioway continued to back the British and many engaged in acts of violence against settlers across the region. Pro-British Ioway warriors joined the Sac and Fox in a series of attacks against settlers in the Boonslick region and continued attacks against the Osage, many of whom had thrown their support behind the United States in the war.

It is difficult to know just how many in the tribe supported Hard Heart or who was among them. There is some evidence that the young headman White Cloud was a member of the group, which apparently included enough fighting men to form an intimidating war party. Captain Horatio Stark, the U.S. commander at Fort Madison, reported in April of 1813 that Hard Heart's son visited the fort to ask permission to launch attacks on pro-British Sac and Fox living nearby. "The Ioways deserve every assistance and I hope [they] will receive it," Stark wrote Benjamin Howard, at that time serving briefly as governor of the Missouri Territory. "It is a just war on their part, and I am induced to believe it unavoidable."

At some point during the war, Hard Heart led his group away from the violence of the Missouri Territory. For a time they found refuge on the west side of the Missouri River with their kinsmen, the Otoe-Missouria. William Clark, who replaced Howard as governor in 1813 and at the same time became superintendent of Indian affairs in St. Louis, advised this move as part of an effort to calm the unstable situation in the eastern portion of the territory. "[The friendly portion of] These Tribes are formidable in number and have for some time past been in a state of poverty," Clark wrote to Secretary of War John Armstrong in September

1813. "If suffered to continue I believe they would join our enemies." To help prevent this, Clark established a trading factory north of the site of the present-day town of Glasgow, Missouri, and encouraged pro-American members of the Ioway and Sac and Fox to move their villages to the region. Clark reported to Armstrong that he had directed the factor at Fort Madison to relocate to this new post to trade with the three tribes. At about that same time, George Sibley, who had been forced to close Fort Osage, opened a trading post at a site near present-day Arrow Rock, primarily to continue business with the Osage, although other tribes frequently visited the post.

Meanwhile, the Indian agent and trader Manuel Lisa enlisted the Yankton Dakota, Omaha, and Osage to fight those Ioway and Sac and Fox who remained stubbornly pro-British. Benjamin Howard reportedly commented that inciting such violence between Indian tribes was "not only justifiable, but good policy." British-backed Ioway raiders stole livestock and destroyed crops. Two of the Ioways' most infamous attacks came after the signing of the Treaty of Ghent, which ended the war in late December 1814. In April 1815, Ioways took part in raids on the settlement of Cote Sans Dessein, near the confluence of the Missouri River and the Osage River, and against Cooper's Fort, near the mouth of the Chariton River. Six settlers, including Captain Sarshall Cooper, were killed in those attacks.

The Ioways' last hope of turning back the oncoming tide of Euro-American immigration died with the defeat of the British in the War of 1812. The United States successfully neutralized a major enemy that had hindered its progress in developing the Missouri Territory. With the British safely out of the picture, only one more obstacle remained between American settlers and the land they so eagerly coveted: the native people who still called the territory home. In 1815, the U.S. military firmly reestablished its foothold in the territory with the reopening of Fort Osage and prepared to focus on overcoming this final barrier to westward expansion.

❀ ❀ ❀

The end of the war and its hostilities cleared the way for wag-onloads of settlers to enter the Missouri Territory on overland trails like the Boonslick Road, which began at St. Charles and extended 140 miles into what is now Howard County, Missouri. In 1817, wagon trains of up to 100 people and stretching almost a mile in length passed through St. Charles on their way west. As the Missouri Territory's nonnative population grew, Indians found themselves becoming uncomfortably outnumbered. William Clark estimated that by 1817 approximately 5,000 native people lived in the territory. That same year Howard County had a population of 1,050 white men and St. Louis, the territorial capital, boasted a population of nearly 3,000. By 1819, the *Missouri Intelligencer* reported that 271 wagons filled mostly with settlers from Kentucky and Tennessee traveled the Boonslick Road in a single month. The entire population of the Missouri Territory grew from 25,000 at the end of the War of 1812 to 66,000 just five years later.

To pave the way for this population explosion, the U.S. government scrambled to secure clear title to all the land within the territory's borders. Though the Osage had ceded their rights to much of the territory in 1808 and settlers had petitioned the government to obtain title to land in the Boonslick country in 1814, the Sac and Fox and Ioway still claimed most of northern Missouri after the war's end.

To secure the land cessions they desired, federal officials first needed to reach permanent peace agreements with the tribes living in the Missouri and Illinois Territories. To accomplish this task, Secretary of War James Monroe appointed trader Auguste Chouteau, Illinois Territorial Governor Ninian Edwards, and Missouri Territorial Governor William Clark to serve as treaty commissioners in March 1815. The commissioners' first order of business was to inform the tribes that the United States and Great Britain had reached an agreement ending the war between them. Second, the commissioners needed to sign formal agreements of peace and friendship with tribes like the Ioway and Sac and Fox that had opposed the United States during the war.

During the summer of 1815, the commissioners met with two thousand leaders from nineteen Indian tribes just north of St. Louis at Portage des Sioux. Their council with the Ioway took place on September 16. On that day, seventeen headmen led by Hard Heart signed an agreement that reestablished friendship between the Ioway nation and the U.S. government. In their report on the council, the commissioners also noted a surprising development. "The Ioways are very desirous of coming more closely under the protection of the United States," wrote the commissioners, "and for this purpose wish to cede a part of their lands in order to obtain annuities like the rest of the neighboring Indian tribes. This is a spontaneous offer on their part, and as the land would be a valuable acquisition on many counts, particularly so in the event of future hostilities, it might be very advisable to accept the proposition."

The government ultimately declined the Ioway offer, but it is difficult to know just why the tribe proposed it. Did the commissioners pressure the Ioway headmen to offer such a proposal, or was it presented freely of their own will? What would make the Ioway wish to part with their land? Were the Ioway leaders who attended the treaty council eager to please the commissioners because they all shared Hard Heart's pro-American position, or did they genuinely feel that they needed the protection and the assistance—financial and otherwise—of the government? Whatever their motivation, it certainly seems possible that the Ioway offer was genuine.

There were clear signs after the War of 1812 that the Ioway people's quality of life was worsening. As William Clark had noted in 1813, the tribe lived in poverty, and its political and military stability was uncertain. The constant violence and upheaval continued after the war years and disrupted the balanced seasonal cycle of tribal life. During these years, the Ioway suffered two devastating attacks from their enemies. The Omaha launched an assault on them in the summer of 1814 that reportedly left the Ioway "annihilated." A year later, Sioux warriors killed twenty-two Ioway and destroyed fields located near the Chariton River in north-central Missouri. As a result of this violence, it grew increasingly more difficult for the Ioway to focus on agriculture and on the seasonal hunting trips that provided them with food and hides for trading.

Perhaps the most telling sign of the Ioways' difficulty was the fact that they remained scattered long after the War of 1812 ended. Clark reported in 1816 that the Ioway primarily lived in two large villages, one inside the Missouri Territory on the Grand River, and the other just north of the territory on the lower Des Moines River. A map of the United States printed that same year by the Philadelphia-based cartographer John Melish located an Ioway village on the Missouri River near the present site of the town of Council Bluffs, Iowa. Melish placed a second village at the mouth of the Iowa River. While these two sources differ in their location of the villages, they agree that two large Ioway villages remained separated by hundreds of miles after the War of 1812 ended.

At the time, some U.S. officials believed this separation meant that the Ioway had broken into opposing factions. Edwin James, who traveled through the region as a member of Major Stephen Long's 1819 expedition, believed that this fracture was the direct result of the tribe's divided loyalties during the War of 1812. "During our late contest with Great Britain," James wrote, "[Hard Heart] turned his back upon his nation, in consequence of their raising the tomahawk upon our citizens." Hard Heart, many believed, had moved his followers away from the main Ioway village on the Des Moines River as an expression of his displeasure with the rest of the tribe.

Another possibility, however, is that the Ioways' split was the result of the continuing depletion of wild game that accompanied the arrival of settlers. As increasing numbers of settlers occupied Ioway hunting land near the Mississippi River, the Sac and Fox also continued to hunt regularly west of the river. As a result, the Ioway were forced to rely more heavily on the land farther west, between the Grand River and Missouri River, for their own hunting. Clark cited the "state of poverty" of the tribes as part of his reason for encouraging them to move west during the war. Ioway headmen may have decided that a portion of the tribe should remain farther west simply because there was not enough game to support the entire nation near the Des Moines River village.

5

Muddled Diplomacy and Military Missteps

At the beginning of the War of 1812, the Missouri Territory had been protected by only three military installations. After complaints about the poor condition of the old Cantonment Bellefontaine on the Missouri River near St. Louis, the secretary of war had approved building a new Fort Bellefontaine on a nearby hill in 1810. The threat of violence had forced the military to abandon Fort Osage in April 1813. American troops also had to abandon their post at Fort Madison on the Mississippi River near the mouth of the Des Moines. Even though troops returned to both forts after the war, American officials realized that if they were to adequately control trade and end violence between settlers and native populations within the territory's borders, they would need to establish a greater military presence.

During the treaty negotiations that took place at Portage des Sioux in 1815, treaty commissioners William Clark, Ninian Edwards, and Auguste Chouteau informed the Indian delegates that the United States planned to increase the military's presence by establishing more forts along the upper Mississippi and the Missouri Rivers. The process began in 1816 when the U.S.

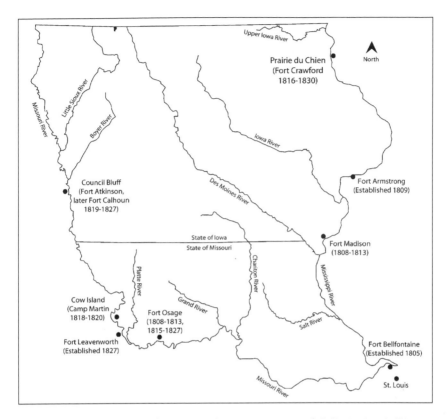

Map of U.S. military forts on the Missouri and Mississippi Rivers, 1805–1830. As the United States sought to gain more control over the Mississippi and Missouri River valleys, a series of military posts and forts was constructed that reached farther into Indian land. (Map by the author.)

government sent troops under the command of Colonel Henry Atkinson north along the Mississippi River to construct a series of forts in territory that the British had controlled before the War of 1812. That summer, detachments replaced the old British fortification at Green Bay and established Fort Crawford at Prairie du Chien. One thousand men led by Brigadier General Thomas A. Smith built an installation called Fort Armstrong on Rock Island at the confluence of the Mississippi and Rock Rivers.

In 1818, Secretary of War John C. Calhoun and Colonel Atkinson developed a plan to send a flotilla of nine keelboats up the Missouri River to transport the First Battalion of the Rifle Regiment from Fort Bellefontaine to the mouth of the Yellowstone River, near the present-day city of Williston, North Dakota. They hoped to complete the journey in time to construct a permanent fort there before winter. The location was important to the United States because it provided a vantage point from which they could monitor the northern Plains Indian population to prevent them from trading with the British. The Yellowstone expedition fell far short of its goal, however. Numerous delays in shipments of equipment and provisions prevented the troops from leaving Fort Bellefontaine until August 30, 1818. Once under way, the expedition proceeded up the Missouri River at a disappointing pace of less than seven and a half miles a day. With cold weather coming on, the flotilla stopped in mid-October to build winter quarters, having traveled just a third of the way to the Yellowstone River.

As cold weather moved in, Atkinson returned to the relative comfort of St. Louis, leaving 260 members of the Yellowstone expedition to spend the winter of 1818–1819 camped on Isle des Vaches, Cow Island, near the present-day town of Iatan in Platte County, Missouri. The soldiers established Camp Martin on the island and erected what one member of the camp called "comfortable winter quarters" in less than a month. According to firsthand accounts, the soldiers seem to have eaten well. Edwin James, who arrived at the island the following spring with Stephen Long's scientific expedition, estimated that the men at the camp killed between two and three thousand deer that winter and also ate an untold number of elk, beaver, bear, and turkey as well as grapes, plums, and honey. When game was scarce, the troops supplemented their diet with beef from the first cattle herd ever driven into the region.

While the hunting may have been good, some of the camp's neighbors proved to be unfriendly. The soldiers' hunting parties, cattle, supply boats, and even Camp Martin itself became irresistible targets for members of the Kansas tribe, who lived south of the island near the present-day site of Kansas City. In an attempt to put an end to the thefts, a detail of soldiers raided a Kansas camp and captured eight men the military suspected of stealing supplies. The soldiers took the men to Camp Martin and three days later tried them on charges of stealing and breaking the treaty of peace the Kansas had made with the United States.

When asked to speak in his own defense at the trial, one of the Kansas men pointed out that his people did not control the actions of their young men in the same way that the U.S. military did. He told his accusers that the Kansas men were as "free as the air which they breathe, light and impetuous as the Antelope. . . . To confine them to one valley," he continued, "would deprive them of their subsistence." He urged the military to allow its own soldiers to live the same way. The accused Kansas asked to be released, but the court found them guilty and punished five of the men by beating them. Even after the trial and the strict punishment of the Kansas, raids on Camp Martin and its soldiers continued throughout the winter.

William Clark, who at this time was serving as both superintendent of Indian affairs and governor of the Missouri Territory, had long been concerned about conflict between native and non-native people in the region. He had urged Secretary of War John C. Calhoun to appoint "an Agent [to] be sent among the numerous Tribes of the Missouri River . . . to check the excesses and disorder . . . and to prevent their continuance." Clark was especially concerned that nonlicensed traders were "misleading and corrupting" the Indians by selling them inferior trade goods and contraband alcohol. He argued that an agent assigned to work specifically with the native people of the Missouri River would help control violence and protect U.S. trade interests in the region. In 1819, Calhoun acted on Clark's request by naming Clark's twenty-six-year-old nephew Benjamin O'Fallon to be the first Indian agent on the Missouri River.

O'Fallon had served as an Indian agent in present-day Minnesota from 1816 to 1818. There, it had been his job to pressure

Benjamin O'Fallon was just twenty-six years old when Secretary of War John C. Calhoun appointed him to be the first Indian agent on the Missouri River in 1819. The nephew of William Clark, the famed explorer and superintendent of Indian affairs in St. Louis, O'Fallon gained a reputation for his strict and sometimes harsh methods of Indian diplomacy. Though his rough tactics earned him the scorn of military men such as Colonel Henry Atkinson and the wary regard of Indian leaders like the Omaha headman Big Elk, O'Fallon held his post as Indian agent until 1827. (Courtesy of the State Historical Society of Missouri, Columbia.)

the Dakota Sioux to end their long-standing trade relationship with the British. When it came to Indian diplomacy, O'Fallon appears to have preferred brute force to gentle persuasion. His efforts with the Dakota Sioux had succeeded largely because of the fifty well-armed infantrymen who had accompanied him into Sioux territory. The rough characteristics that defined his professional life extended into his civilian life, and on at least one occasion got him into trouble in St. Louis. In May 1818, a court had convicted and fined O'Fallon and his brother John one thousand dollars for committing "assaults on citizens on the Election ground."

Accompanying Atkinson's expedition as it continued up the river, Major O'Fallon's first order of business as Indian agent of the Missouri River was to meet with various Indian nations along the way and establish formal relations with them. Calhoun had expressed hope that O'Fallon would be both firm and fair in his dealing with the Indians. He was to inform the nations that they must deal exclusively with the United States in matters of trade and war. "Undoubtedly the Indians ought to be fully impressed with our capacity to avenge any injury which they may offer us; but it is no less important that they should be equally impressed with our justice and humanity. Should you succeed in convincing them of both, all difficulties will be removed."

The zealous O'Fallon continued his heavy-handed methods of persuasion as he proceeded upriver with Colonel Atkinson in June 1819. In one of his first meetings with the Otoe and the Omaha, he made a show of severely punishing a man who had boasted about taking part in the 1812 attack on U.S. soldiers at Fort Dearborn on the Chicago River. O'Fallon avenged the attack by cutting off the man's ears, giving him one hundred lashes, and throwing his weapons in the river.

Word of the agent's rogue style of diplomacy preceded him as he traveled up the Missouri River. When the Omaha headman Big Elk met with O'Fallon, he warily inquired about the motive behind his methods. "We have heard of your tying up and whipping individuals of several nations, as you ascended this river. What is the offense which will subject us to this punishment? I wish to know, that I may inform my people, that they may be on their guard."

While O'Fallon's actions quickly earned him Henry Atkinson's contempt, he was just one of many professional challenges that Atkinson faced in 1819. After the disappointing progress of the Yellowstone expedition the previous year, Atkinson was eager to make a second effort to push his troops to their destination. To accomplish this, the War Department had expanded the expedition, by then called the Missouri expedition, to include the Sixth Infantry Regiment. The infantry had arrived in St. Louis in the spring of 1819 and was prepared to follow Atkinson up the river to join the Rifle Regiment at Camp Martin. The War Department contracted to have supplies transported on five steamboats—the first ever to be used on such a mission on the dangerous and shallow Missouri River.

Secretary of War Calhoun had also ordered a scientific expedition, commanded by Major Stephen Long of the Corps of Engineers, to accompany the Sixth Infantry. Long's crew of scientists included botanist William Baldwin, zoologist Thomas Say, artist Samuel Seymour, geologist Augustus E. Jessup, and naturalist and artist Titian Ramsey Peale. The small group traveled upriver in a small stern-wheeled steamboat that Long designed and named the *Western Engineer*. Because of its unusual appearance, members of the expedition expected the *Western Engineer* to generate excitement and attention from native and nonnative people alike. "The bow of this vessel exhibits the form of a huge serpent, black and scaly, rising out of the water from under the boat," wrote a reporter for *Niles' Weekly Register*. "[H]is head [is] as high as the deck, darting forward, his mouth open, vomiting smoke, and apparently carrying the boat on its back." Perhaps even more impressive than the *Western Engineer's* ornate bow were the artillery pieces on its deck. Peale, who had drawn sketches of the boat, noted in his

Major Stephen Long of the Corps of Engineers commanded the scientific branch of the 1819 Missouri expedition, leading a group that included a botanist, zoologist, naturalist, artist, and geologist. Though the members of the expedition intended to travel to the mouth of the Yellowstone River near the border between present-day North Dakota and Montana, they spent the winter of 1819–1820 at Council Bluff before turning west to explore the Great Plains. (Courtesy of the State Historical Society of Missouri, Columbia.)

journal that its "arms consist of one brass four-pounder mounted on the bow, four brass 2 7/8 inch howitzers, two on swivels, and two on field carriages, [and] two wolf pieces carrying four ounce balls."

Even as it prepared to depart from Fort Bellefontaine, Atkinson's flotilla experienced problems. Both the steamboats and Colonel James Johnson, the contractor hired to supply the expedition, proved unreliable. Johnson failed to deliver supplies and food to the troops in time for their scheduled departure. Of the five steamboats that he planned to use to carry men and supplies, two broke down even before reaching Fort Bellefontaine. After long delays, Long's scientists finally departed Bellefontaine on the *Western Engineer* in late June 1819. Johnson's three remaining steamboats and several keelboats carrying members of the Sixth Infantry left the fort on July 4 and 5.

Progress on the river, which usually ran low during the summer months, proved painfully slow and difficult for the expedition. In many places, the river was so shallow that the men had to attach ropes to the boats and pull them upstream. Because the detachment had to set out before Johnson could deliver some of the necessary food and supplies, the exhausted men were forced to hunt for their food and often went hungry. On July 14, John Gale, a military doctor traveling with the flotilla, noted in his journal that after several "failures" of the contractor, "our subsistence is precarious." The enlisted men soon became so disgruntled that the officers had to physically restrain several who attempted to desert and return to St. Louis.

Thirty miles below the town of Franklin, in Howard County, one of Johnson's supply boats, the *Jefferson,* became the first steamboat to sink on the Missouri River. The remaining boats experienced numerous mechanical breakdowns, many of which were caused by bits of fine sand blowing into the engines.

At Franklin four members of Long's crew, Say, Jessup, Seymour, and O'Fallon's interpreter John Dougherty, bought pack horses and traveled overland to Fort Osage. While the rest of the members of the expedition struggled to navigate the boats through the shallow, snag-filled river, the small party had time to explore the surrounding landscape. They visited Arrow Rock, a well-known landmark where for centuries Indians from many tribes obtained flint for their arrows. From there they ferried across the Missouri River and investigated a salt works on the Lamine River before rejoining the rest of the expedition at the fort in early August. The flotilla remained at Fort Osage, then considered to be the last outpost of American civilization on the Missouri River, for more than a week to rest, repair the steam engines, and wait for provisions before moving on.

Finally, after fifty grueling days, the struggling procession reached the Rifle Regiment at Camp Martin in mid-August. Upon their arrival at Cow Island, members of the Sixth Infantry discovered that conditions at the Rifle Regiment's camp were not much better than those they had experienced on the river. The game that had been so plentiful through the winter of 1818–1819 had thinned out by spring, forcing the soldiers to travel as far as fifty miles from the island to hunt. During these hunting trips fighting often broke out between the riflemen and native hunting parties. In April 1819 a group of Ioway and Otoe men had attacked a group of hunters led by the Rifle Regiment's quartermaster, Lieutenant Martin Palmer. The Indians took the contents of the canoe in which Palmer's men were traveling. They briefly held one of the riflemen captive and robbed him of his clothing and fifty dollars. A group of seventy men set out from Camp Martin to apprehend the robbers. After three days of searching, the soldiers met a party of Osage in pursuit of the same band of Ioway and Otoe, who had also stolen some horses from the Osage. The riflemen gave the Osage ammunition, helped them cross the Missouri River, and encouraged them to attack the Ioway and Otoe on their behalf should they have the opportunity. In June, Lieutenant Gabriel Field finally captured and punished five Indians he believed had participated in the attack on Palmer's men.

Resolving this and similar incidents involving the soldiers and the Kansas, Pawnee, Ioway, and Otoe kept O'Fallon busy from the moment he reached Cow Island. On August 24, 1819, O'Fallon held a council in which he accused more than 150 Kansas of ill treatment of the soldiers and demanded that they stop harassing them. However, as if to signal the Indians' widespread resistance to the U.S. military, on the same day a large group of Pawnee attacked, robbed, and temporarily held hostage a hunting party of Long's scientists near the camp.

The *Western Engineer* as drawn by Titian Peale in 1819. Of the four steamboats that left Fort Bellefontaine as part of the Missouri expedition in the summer of 1819, the *Western Engineer* was the only one to successfully reach Council Bluff, the site of the expedition's winter camp near present-day Fort Calhoun, Nebraska. Because of its unusual appearance, the *Western Engineer* generated much attention from native and nonnative people alike. "The bow of this vessel exhibits the form of a huge serpent, black and scaly," reported one newspaper correspondent who saw it. Peale also noted that the deck of the boat was outfitted with four brass howitzer guns and two "wolf pieces" that shot four-ounce balls. (Courtesy of the American Philosophical Society.)

After a month of preparation, Atkinson's combined expedition forces, which then numbered about five hundred men, left Camp Martin on September 5, 1819, in a procession that included sixteen keelboats and the *Western Engineer*. For the second year in a row, the expedition had been frustrated in its effort to reach the Yellowstone River. As an impatient U.S. Congress threatened to withdraw funding for the mission,

Atkinson set his sights on traveling just 130 miles farther before winter weather set in. This final leg of the journey took the ill-fated Missouri expedition to Council Bluff, the site of Lewis and Clark's 1804 meeting with the Otoe, and directly through the heart of the Ioways' newly established home.

By the fall of 1819, the scarcity of game on the Des Moines River and a bloody war with the Sac and Fox had forced most Ioway to move to the lands between the Missouri and Platte Rivers in what is now northwest Missouri. After the War of 1812, the Ioway had hunted regularly in the region of the Grand and Chariton River valleys for a time. However, as the region became part of the new Missouri Territory, the Ioway soon found an increasing number of American settlers moving into their hunting grounds. In February 1819, Hard Heart and another Ioway headman named Crane visited George Sibley at Fort Osage to remind him of their claim to the land north of the Missouri River and to ask him to present their case before the U.S. government. They argued that if the Americans would not allow the Ioway to have access to the land, then they should at least compensate them for it with government annuities and assistance.

"I confess myself an advocate for the Ioways in this matter," Sibley wrote to William Clark. "Perhaps it would be just to say, that the forests and wilds of the Missouri belong in common to those Nations of Indians who live contiguous to them, and Hunt thro' them. And that when our [government] thinks proper to reclaim those wilds for the use of our People, remuneration ought to be made in common to those Tribes whose natural pursuits are thus interfered with."

As they struggled to reestablish their claims to land in the Missouri Territory, the Ioway began to feel unwelcome in the region of their Des Moines River villages. Before the War of 1812 the Ioway and the Sac and Fox had joined together to work lead mines in the vicinity of present-day Dubuque, Iowa. The mines proved profitable and allowed the Indians to maintain their

Black Hawk, as drawn by J. O. Lewis in 1855, and, on the following page, Pashepaho, as painted by George Catlin. These two leaders of the Sac and Fox are credited with leading a devastating surprise raid on the Ioway's main village in present-day Van Buren County, Iowa, in May 1819. While the number of Ioway casualties has never been confirmed, many believe that the raid drove the Ioway from the village and into the Missouri River valley. (Images courtesy of the State Historical Society of Missouri, Columbia.)

trade activity even as beaver pelts became scarce. However, the Sac and Fox cut the Ioway out of the mining operation and established a village on their hunting land in 1818; the Ioway retaliated with a series of attacks on their former partners, leading to continued bloodshed.

The Sac and Fox leader Black Hawk later remembered that during those battles "Our young men had repeatedly killed

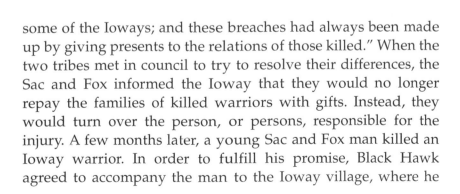

some of the Ioways; and these breaches had always been made up by giving presents to the relations of those killed." When the two tribes met in council to try to resolve their differences, the Sac and Fox informed the Ioway that they would no longer repay the families of killed warriors with gifts. Instead, they would turn over the person, or persons, responsible for the injury. A few months later, a young Sac and Fox man killed an Ioway warrior. In order to fulfill his promise, Black Hawk agreed to accompany the man to the Ioway village, where he

As a young man in the days when Europeans and Americans did not yet outnumber native people, the Ioway leader MaxúThka, or White Cloud, had believed that it was possible to resist them. However, as he approached middle age and settlers flooded into the Missouri Territory, White Cloud understood that it was no longer possible for the Ioway to live the traditional life they once enjoyed on the open prairies. In 1824 he cosigned the first treaty to cede Ioway land to the United States. That same year he agreed to send Ioway boys to study at St. Regis, a Jesuit school located in Florissant, Missouri. (Courtesy of the State Historical Society of Missouri, Columbia.)

Like the Ioway leader White Cloud, the Omaha headman
UnmpaTanga, or Big Elk, had to contend with a world that was rapidly
changing as white settlement in the Missouri River valley threatened
traditional native culture. In an effort to help his people through this
transition, Big Elk tried to befriend and accommodate the whites. He
once told the Indian agent John Dougherty that his esteem for white
people was so strong that he believed that he would become a white
man himself. (Courtesy of the State Historical Society of Missouri,
Columbia.)

would turn him over for punishment. On the day they had planned to go the young man was too sick to travel, so his brother offered to go in his place. When they came within sight of the Ioway village, the killer's brother walked into the village alone, singing his death song as he sat on the ground among the lodges. An Ioway leader rode out to meet Black Hawk, who told him the man had come in place of his sick brother.

As Black Hawk and his party made their way home, they were surprised to hear the sound of horses coming from the direction of the Ioway village. As he prepared to defend himself, Black Hawk was relieved to see that the sound was made by the killer's brother and two horses. "He told me," Black Hawk later recalled, "that after we left him, [the Ioway] menaced him with death for some time—then gave him something to eat—smoked the pipe with him—and made him a present of two horses and some goods and started him after us." Black Hawk said the Sac and Fox were so impressed with the Ioways' conduct that "not one of their people has been killed since by any of our nation."

According to the oral history of the region's first white settlers, however, violence between the Ioway and Sac and Fox reached a tragic climax in May 1819. According to this popular story, Black Hawk and another Sac and Fox headman, Pashepaho, led a surprise attack on a large Ioway village, known as Iowaville, on the Des Moines River near the present-day town of Selma, Iowa. Because the Ioway were outside of their village celebrating a successful buffalo hunt, the Sac and Fox caught most of the villagers unarmed, and a mile or more from their lodges. Some nineteenth-century accounts estimated that the Ioway lost as many as one-third of their total population of fifteen hundred men, women, and children in the attack.

While the story of this attack has remained popular for nearly two centuries, the facts surrounding it are unproved. Black Hawk not only failed to mention the attack in his autobiography but also stated that his people's admiration for the Ioway people led them to stop killing them prior to 1819. A trader named James H. Jordan, however, claimed the Sac and Fox leader had described the attack to him shortly before he died. Jordan in turn reported the incident to the historian A. R. Fulton in the 1880s. He said that the Sac and Fox leader could not determine the number of Ioway killed, but believed that the number was staggering. Jordan added that when he moved to the site nearly a decade after the incident, he could still see graves of the Ioway dead.

A brief account written by an amateur Italian explorer, Giacomo Beltrami, hints that the Dakota Sioux may have been responsible for the massacre of the Ioway. Beltrami traveled up the Mississippi River in 1823 in a failed attempt to be the first white person to identify its source. As he passed the mouth of the Des Moines River, he noted that "This river is inhabited by the Ioways who have been almost all destroyed by the Dakotas."

Most modern historians and archaeologists who have studied the village site and the nineteenth-century population figures for the Ioway are skeptical about the reports of the massacre at Iowaville. The lack of reliable evidence for a large-scale attack leads many to doubt that the Ioway actually suffered losses as large as those that Jordan reported.

Regardless of the number of Ioway dead, it appears that war with the Sac and Fox forced the tribe to abandon the village site and settle near the Missouri River, probably in the spring of 1819. By the time Atkinson's men landed at Council Bluff in September 1819, Benjamin O'Fallon reported, "A Misunderstanding having lately taken place between the Sackees and the Ioways has induced the latter to abandon their original residence (on the Demoin and Mississipi [sic]) and locate themselves on this [Missouri] river," where they were once again living near their relatives the Otoe and Missouria.

After their move, the Ioway were generally living and hunting along the east side of the Missouri River between the Kansas River, at the site of present-day Kansas City, and the western Platte River, near present-day Omaha. The boundaries of the Ioways' land were largely defined by the enemies that surrounded them: the Osage and the Kansas on the south, the Pawnee on the west, the Omaha and Dakota Sioux on the northwest, the Sac and Fox on the northeast, and, perhaps the most worrisome of all, the citizens of the Missouri Territory to the east.

Several members of the newly relocated Ioway happened to be conducting business at Manuel Lisa's trading establishment just below Council Bluff when Atkinson, Long, and their flotilla arrived on September 17, 1819. David Meriwether was a nineteen-year-old sutler, or private supply contractor, who had traveled ahead of the expedition. Years later he recalled that he was standing on shore with some of the Ioway when they noticed the *Western Engineer,* the first steam-powered boat to travel the Missouri River above Cow Island, noisily approaching from downstream. In an attempt to capitalize on what he assumed was the Ioways' ignorance, Meriwether tried to convince them that the approaching craft was in fact a large snake carrying a boat on its back. The Ioway expressed some skepticism about this. Nevertheless, when the boat landed near them and howled as the engines let off steam, they moved away cautiously.

Probably much more unsettling to the Ioway than the appearance of the steam-belching *Western Engineer* was the arrival of the five hundred U.S. soldiers who followed it. Over the next few days, soldiers swarmed the banks of the river at the foot of Council Bluff, felling trees from a nearby stand of timber and quarrying stone from a limestone bluff to build their winter quarters.

As work on the camp progressed, Major O'Fallon sent out messengers to summon members of nearby tribes, the Otoe, Missouria, and Ioway, to a council on October 3 to address their recent fighting with the Pawnee and Omaha. As the council opened, the Indian delegates honored their hosts with traditional songs and dances. After the ceremony, O'Fallon delivered a stern warning to the tribes, telling them if they were not able

During the War of 1812, the Indian agent and trader Manuel Lisa enlisted several Indian tribes to attack those Ioway and Sac and Fox warriors who fought on the side of the British. By 1819 many Ioway frequented Lisa's trading establishment, which was located at the base of Council Bluff near present-day Fort Calhoun, Nebraska. (Courtesy of the State Historical Society of Missouri, Columbia.)

to live together peacefully, the U.S. government would bring in enough soldiers to force them to cease their fighting. He closed his speech by encouraging the delegates to return to their camps for the evening and discuss the need for a lasting peace. O'Fallon asked each tribe to return the next morning with a response to his ultimatum. In his journal of the expedition,

Edwin James reported that as the council ended for the day one group of Ioway refused to return to their camp. Apparently unhappy that they had not been allowed to express their views, several Ioway remained seated until the Otoe headman Ietan chased them away with threats of physical violence.

On the second day of the council, the Otoe and Missouria said they would agree to O'Fallon's demands. When it came time for the Ioway to respond, the headman White Cloud stood to speak. Expecting Hard Heart alone to represent the Ioway in the council, O'Fallon turned his back on White Cloud. When the headman asked why, the agent replied that he "had not come to hear boys talk but to listen to the chiefs of each tribe." Unshaken, White Cloud held his ground. In his memoirs written years later, David Meriwether recalled that the Ioway leader, who was actually older than O'Fallon by nearly a decade, challenged the government's right to interfere in intertribal disputes. "My brother [O'Fallon] said he would force us to make peace with the Pawnees," Meriwether quoted White Cloud as saying.

> Now this is a question between Redmen and in which the white man has no right to interfere, but I will say to you that my tribe will not consent to make peace with the Pawnees. The Great Spirit has placed this broad river [pointing to the Missouri] between us, and woe to the Pawnees who cross it. I know that we are not able to cope with the whites. I have seen some of your soldiers and know that they have better guns than we have, and I am told they are numerous as the sands on the riverbank or the great herds of buffalo on the prairies, but if the whites compel us to make peace with the Pawnees, we will, if we can do no better, scratch you with our toe and finger nails and gnaw you with our teeth. Now my brother has our answer.

With that, White Cloud stalked boldly out of the council, followed by several Ioway delegates.

Historians generally interpret the refusal of some Ioway to

leave the council on the first day and White Cloud's insistence on addressing O'Fallon directly on the second day as signs of a power struggle between White Cloud and the tribe's U.S.-appointed spokesman, Hard Heart. However, there appears to be little evidence to support the existence of a rivalry between the two leaders. Both headmen supported the Americans during the War of 1812, and it appears that White Cloud moved west—away from the violence—with Hard Heart during the war years. While there clearly was some sort of disagreement among the Ioway who attended the council, it may have been prompted by internal differences or by their respect for the tribal council tradition in which all the Ioway headmen considered and openly discussed all viewpoints concerning matters affecting the life of the tribe.

With the coming of cold weather, the thoughts of both the Indian nations and the U.S. troops living near Council Bluff quickly turned from diplomacy toward the basic need for food and shelter. As the soldiers hurried to complete their quarters and secure enough food for the winter, the natives living along the river worried about the effect that an additional five hundred soldiers would have on the region's supply of wild game. The Omaha headman Big Elk expressed his concerns to Major O'Fallon when they met on October 14. "My nation is coming down here to hunt this winter," Big Elk told the agent, "and if you send out your soldiers to hunt also, they will drive off all the game, and our women and children will starve."

As winter progressed, Big Elk's concerns seemed well founded. Thick ice on the Missouri River near Cow Island prevented a boat loaded with much-needed food, medicine, and supplies from reaching the encampment at Council Bluff. Though the men were generally able to secure sufficient amounts of meat, they were almost totally without vegetables and fruit. By January, the surgeon John Gale reported that scurvy had become a serious problem and that many of the enlisted men were "sickly." Eager to recover the supplies from the stranded supply boat, Atkinson chose David Meriwether to lead a party of five soldiers to Cow Island and retrieve as many supplies as possible. With White Cloud as their guide, the men braved snow and temperatures as low as 26 degrees below zero to successfully complete the 260-mile round trip in twenty-seven days. Despite the arrival of supplies, which included iodine to treat scurvy, and Meriwether's success in trading two barrels of watered-down whiskey to the Omaha in exchange for fifty bushels of dried corn, soldiers began to die in the camp. By spring, scurvy had claimed 160, or about one-third of the camp's population.

While the suffering of the soldiers during the winter of 1819–1820 is well documented, that which the Ioway and neighboring tribes must have endured is not. The surviving journals of those connected with the Long expedition reported a scarcity of food in the Missouri River valley, noting that the tribes near Council Bluff were hungry. Edwin James reported that the soldiers' hunting parties sometimes came back to camp empty-handed. After traveling more than sixty miles up the Little Sioux River, one group returned having seen only one buffalo. James also noted that in January some Omaha had been accused of raiding Pawnee cache pits. Meanwhile, another group of Omaha joined the Dakota for a trip up the Boyer River, far into present-day Iowa, to retrieve dried oats the Dakota had stored in their cache pits. In March, Big Elk stopped to visit soldiers at Council Bluff. He asked the men if they thought it was strange that his people were traveling the countryside and not home, safe in their lodges in the cold of winter. "Our poverty and necessities," he told them, "compel us to do so in pursuit of game."

The U.S. government had intended the small post at Council Bluff, which they named Fort Atkinson, to calm the unstable atmosphere that existed near the Missouri Territory's western border. In many ways, however, it had the opposite effect because the presence of the military created a new set of problems. The Ioway and their neighbors deeply resented the permanent settlement of white soldiers and the negative effect it had on their land, most noticeably, the dramatic decrease in wild game around the fort. In 1823, the German Duke Paul Wilhelm of Wuerttemberg reported that "the [bison] have not been seen [near the Platte River valley] for years, having been frightened away by the military establishment at the Council Bluffs."

The troops also changed the character of the landscape around them. They cleared trees and quarried stone to use for building and introduced herds of cattle, with their destructive grazing habits, into the environment. The presence of the military also helped open the way for increased settlement. Soldiers from the fort surveyed at least two new major overland trails to accommodate the need to move more people and supplies into the region. Field's Trace connected Council Bluff with the lower Grand River in the Missouri Territory, and a second new trail ran between Fort Atkinson and Camp Coldwater, later called Fort Snelling, three hundred miles to the northeast at the site of present-day St. Paul, Minnesota.

Perhaps most troublesome to the Ioway, as the scolding White Cloud delivered to Major O'Fallon at Council Bluff suggests, was the government's attempts to interfere in their tribal affairs and intertribal conflicts. In a letter to Secretary of War Calhoun in April 1821, O'Fallon admitted that there was little the troops could do for the time being to overcome native resistance. The agent reported that while the troops had impressed the Indians, they were "still disposed to underrate our strength, to believe that the detachment of troops on the Missouri is not a part, but the whole of our Army."

6

Navigating the White Road

By 1820, many of the Ioway were resigned to the overwhelming presence of the *Ma'unke*, or white people, and ready to make concessions to the government of the United States. The fortunes of their once-thriving nation had fallen significantly during the first two decades of the nineteenth century. With their small population diminished by war and disease, the Ioway were in no position to effectively resist the more than sixty-six thousand white settlers who called the Missouri Territory home by 1820, or to protect themselves from the aggressions of neighboring tribes. Moving often to avoid hostilities, they could not maintain their traditional annual cycle of hunting and farming. This hindered their ability to produce their own food and to obtain the hides that they traded for other necessities. Increasingly poor and facing starvation, the Ioway people had scattered into several small bands to scratch out a meager existence between the Grand and Missouri Rivers.

When the Missouri territorial legislature completed its first state constitution in 1820, it called for a state boundary line that cut the Ioways' homeland in half. According to its constitution, the northern half of the proposed new state would be defined by a line that extended one hundred miles due north from the confluence of the Kansas and Missouri Rivers at the site that would one day become Kansas City. From the western tip of that line, the border would run east to the Des Moines River and then follow the Des Moines to the Mississippi River. Missouri's petition for statehood had been held up for three years as Congress debated the question of whether it would be admitted as a free or slave state. When the request finally passed and Missouri entered the Union as a slave state on August 10, 1821, many Ioway were living within its boundaries.

The Reverend Jedediah Morse, a Connecticut minister who was interested in improving the welfare of Indians, reported to the secretary of war in 1822 that the various Ioway groups moved so often it was hard to determine where they were all living. It was during this period of upheaval that some Ioway unsuccessfully attempted to live again near their former village on the Des Moines River. Despite the fact that the Sac and Fox had gained control of the region, it retained an important place in the Ioways' culture. Spiritually, the land around the village site remained sacred to the Ioway as the final resting place of generations of their ancestors. Economically, the site was important because it was the location of the summer fields they had cultivated for decades. In the crowded valley of the lower Missouri River they had no permanent villages or fields and were always on the move looking for food.

Duff Green, an early resident of Chariton County, noted that the Ioway resented the situation and wondered why the U.S. government was unable to assist them. As a brigadier general in the First Division of the Missouri Militia, it was Green's job to ensure the safety of both whites and natives inside the state's borders. He believed that if the secretary of war assigned an agent to work directly with the Ioway, it would improve their situation and make them less likely to strike out against settlers or other tribes. He noted that the Ioways' recent move away from the agent assigned to them on the Des Moines River "has

When Missouri achieved statehood in 1821, its first two U.S. senators, Thomas Hart Benton (above) and David Barton (following page), served on the Congressional Committee on Indian Affairs. Later, in 1829, Benton led the campaign to enlarge the state by annexing the Platte River region, located on the Missouri's northwest border. The land "is essential to the State of Missouri," declared Benton, "and hardly desirable to the Indians." (Images courtesy of the State Historical Society of Missouri, Columbia.)

heretofore placed [them] without the immediate superinten-
dence of any of the regularly appointed agents of the
Government."

After Missouri achieved statehood, its first two U.S. senators,
Thomas Hart Benton and David Barton, demanded that the
state's settlers and fur-trading interests be protected from
Indian violence. Both Benton and Barton served on the
Congressional Committee on Indian Affairs, and they recognized that the growth of Missouri would be hampered until the
federal government could settle the claims that the Ioway and
the Sac and Fox held over portions of the state that lay north of
the Missouri River and west of the Mississippi River. The senators echoed Green's plea for a greater number of agents to act as
liaisons between the government and individual tribes on the
lower Missouri River, like the Osage, Kansas, Sac and Fox,

Dakota, and Ioway. The senators recognized that Indian agent Benjamin O'Fallon's increasing preoccupation with Missouri River tribes living north of Council Bluff made him unable to give those tribes living on Missouri's western and northern borders the attention they deserved. Barton and Benton urged Secretary of War Calhoun to recruit "men in the vigor of their ages and of sufficient weight of character to command the respect of the white people and of the Indians" to become Indian agents on the Missouri frontier. But despite the senators' urgings, it would be three more years before Calhoun selected Martin Palmer to be the Ioways' first agent in March 1825.

In the summer of 1823 Hard Heart died in a battle with the Yankton Dakota. While many had doubted Thomas Jefferson's wisdom in recognizing him as the chief headman of the Ioway in 1809, Hard Heart had proved to be a dependable U.S. ally. He had successfully prevented some Ioway from siding against the United States during the War of 1812 and had maintained that alliance among most of the Ioway in the years after the war. A veteran of fifty battles, Hard Heart was a strong defender of his people and of his personal pride. He once came to blows in a heated argument with the Otoe headman Ietan. On another occasion he unsuccessfully challenged to a duel an American army captain he believed had cheated him.

But Hard Heart also defied many of the negative views that nineteenth-century Europeans and Americans had of Indian people. Edwin James, who had been a member of Stephen Long's 1819 scientific expedition, admired the Ioway headman for his intelligence and for his extensive knowledge of white culture. James recalled that Hard Heart was fluent in English and had once surprised Indian agent John Dougherty by quizzing him about astronomy and the nature of the earth's orbit around the sun.

After Hard Heart's death, White Cloud succeeded him as the U.S. government's favored Ioway headman. White Cloud had become an Ioway leader at a young age after his father, Wounding

Arrow, was killed in a surprise attack as he feasted in the lodge of a Dakota Sioux headman. The Ioway sent out a war party to avenge Wounding Arrow's death. In the battle that followed, White Cloud showed his bravery by jumping from his horse and fighting his enemies on foot. He earned his first battle honors by taking the scalp of the Dakota leader who had led his father into the ambush. Though he was middle-aged at the time of Hard Heart's death, the six-feet, two-inch White Cloud still possessed the commanding figure of a warrior. After Commissioner of Indian Affairs Thomas McKenney met White Cloud in Washington in 1824, he remarked that the Ioway leader "possessed great bodily strength and activity, and was a man of perfect symmetry of person, and of uncommon beauty."

Paul Wilhelm, Duke of Wuerttemberg, reported that most Ioway were "in deep mourning" because of the loss of Hard Heart and their defeat by the Yankton Dakota. Wilhelm may have been referring to White Cloud when he continued, "[the Ioway] are under a new leader, who at times seems to be their priest." From the U.S. point of view, the transition between Hard Heart and White Cloud was a smooth one. Both leaders had generally cooperated with the United States and proved to be dependable supporters of its policies. Experience had taught White Cloud to be pragmatic in his dealings with the whites. McKenney reported that White Cloud had expressed regret for his participation in the gun battle in which the French traders Joseph Merachal and Joseph Tebeau had died in 1808. White Cloud told McKenney that he had promised William Clark that he would never again fight against the whites and that his heart was at peace.

White Cloud understood that it was no longer possible for the Ioway people to resist white settlement, and he supported the government's efforts to train the native people of the lower Missouri River valley to live, farm, and govern themselves in the same way that the white people did. In an attempt to ally the Ioway more closely with the United States and to secure the help that they needed from the government, White Cloud agreed to the first sale of Ioway land. In 1824, William Clark, as superintendent of Indian affairs in St. Louis, summoned White Cloud and another Ioway headman, Great Walker, to Washington, D.C., with a delegation of Ioway, Sac and Fox, and Piankeshaw to meet with President James Monroe. Clark arranged the council in hopes of ending the increasingly hostile atmosphere on Missouri's western border. Monroe not only planned to require the Ioway to renew their vows of loyalty to the United States but also wanted to make possible the cession of all Ioway land within the State of Missouri.

While in the capital city, government officials entertained the Indians at a number of Washington social events where White Cloud's wife, Female Flying Pigeon, became an object of fascination among the city's social elite. White Cloud, on the other hand, drew unwanted attention to himself when he suffered a broken arm in a drunken fall from a second-story window of the Indian Queen Hotel. The delegates visited factories and a shipyard and had their portraits painted by the noted artist Charles Bird King.

When the delegation met in council in early August with President Monroe and Commissioner McKenney, it was clear that disagreements over land fueled much of the conflict between the Ioway and Sac and Fox. The Sac and Fox delegation, led by Keokuk, began the meeting by questioning the right of the Osage to give up their claim to "all lands situated northwardly of the river Missouri" as part of their 1808 treaty since it was the Sac and Fox who controlled that land. The Ioway headmen countered that the Sac and Fox had no claim to northern Missouri either, nor, for that matter, did the United States. Treaty documents show that when he addressed the president, White Cloud had pointed out that the Ioway had been "deceived by the Spaniards and the French for they had no right to the country which they sold to the Americans." Recognizing, however, that their people did not have the power to challenge the United States for possession of the land, White Cloud and Great Walker agreed to sell all Ioway rights to the northern half of Missouri for five thousand dollars. The treaty also promised the tribe a blacksmith, agricultural tools, and cattle, which the government hoped would encourage the Ioway to devote themselves to agriculture and allow them to become self-sufficient once again.

Instead of solving problems, the Treaty of 1824 seemed to compound them for the Ioway by further fragmenting the tribe. Soon after returning to the Missouri River from Washington, Great Walker expressed deep regret over his role in signing away the tribe's land. The Ioway leader, whom McKenney described as "morose and sour," claimed not to have understood the treaty. Blackening his face as a sign of mourning, Great Walker vowed to continue to occupy the ceded land and to ignore the treaty's order that the Ioway vacate it by January 1, 1826.

White Cloud was camped along the Platte River near the present-day town of Agency, Missouri, where a new agency for the Ioway was about to be established. Great Walker, meanwhile, led a group of Ioway to north-central Missouri to live along the Grand and Chariton Rivers. This move not only showed a split between the two influential tribal leaders, who had once been so close that they referred to each other as brothers, but also was yet another division in the allegiances of the Ioway people.

If the Treaty of 1824 helped to further divide the Ioway people, it also did little to end intertribal fighting over land. Less than six months after the council, the nations that signed it were fighting once again. In July 1825 in an effort to end the warfare, William Clark called more than one thousand representatives of the Chippewa, Winnebago, Menominee, Ottawa, Potawatomi, Dakota, Ioway, and Sac and Fox to a treaty council at Prairie du Chien, at the confluence of the Mississippi and Wisconsin Rivers. Clark's primary objective in organizing the council was to persuade the tribes to establish boundaries for the land they claimed. In an attempt to stop the serious violence between the Dakota and the Sac and Fox, Clark successfully proposed a

Much of the conflict that took place between the Ioway and the Sac and Fox had to do with their competition to control land in what is now southern Iowa and northern Missouri. Disputes over land led to an argument between the Sac and Fox leader Keokuk and the Ioway head-man White Cloud when the two visited Washington, D.C., to negotiate the Treaty of 1824. Though each leader felt that his people had exclusive rights to the northern half of the state of Missouri, they both agreed to relinquish their claims to that land to the United States as part of the treaty. (Lithograph of Keokuk by J. O. Lewis, reproduction courtesy of the State Historical Society of Missouri, Columbia.)

White Cloud's wife, Rut'ánweMi, or Female Flying Pigeon, accompanied the Ioway delegation that traveled to the capital city to negotiate the Treaty of 1824. As part of their tour government officials led the Indians to several tourist sites and entertained them at a number of Washington social events, where Female Flying Pigeon became a favorite among the city's social elite. (Courtesy of the State Historical Society of Missouri, Columbia.)

In July 1825, William Clark, superintendent of Indian affairs in St. Louis, called more than one thousand representatives of the Chippewa, Winnebago, Menominee, Ottawa, Potawatomi, Dakota, Ioway, and Sac and Fox to a treaty council at Prairie du Chien, at the confluence of the Mississippi and Wisconsin Rivers. Clark's primary objective in convening the council was to persuade the tribes to establish boundaries for the land they claimed and to convince them not to violate those boundaries once they were agreed upon. (Etching of the Treaty of 1825 by J. O. Lewis, reproduction courtesy of the State Historical Society of Missouri, Columbia.)

twenty-mile-wide line of "neutral ground" that ran southwest from the junction of the upper Iowa and Mississippi Rivers. He directed the Ioway to share the land between the neutral ground and the Missouri border with the Sac and Fox until another council could be held to sort out their respective claims.

Just before signing the Treaty of 1824 White Cloud and Great Walker had made another significant step toward integrating their people into Euro-American culture. The two headmen agreed to send Ioway boys to study at St. Regis, a new school established by Jesuits in May 1824 at Florissant, Missouri, near St. Louis. On June 11, as they prepared to depart from St. Louis for their trip to Washington, the two Ioway headmen and Indian agent Gabriel Vasques delivered five boys, including Great Walker's twelve-year-old son, whom the Jesuits called Peter, to St. Regis. At the time of their arrival, the only students at the school were two Sac and Fox boys who had arrived less than a month earlier.

Though Father Pierre-Jean DeSmet, who was a young teacher at St. Regis in 1824, described the Ioway boys as "very attentive," they apparently did not adapt easily to life at the school. Shortly after their arrival, two of the Ioway boys escaped and managed to travel five miles on foot before priests from the schools caught up with them. Adjusting to the daily schedule of the school proved difficult for the students. Father Charles Felix Van Quickenborne, who established St. Regis, later recalled that the boys had to work in the fields each day for several hours. Farming did not appeal to them because it was traditionally the work of native women and children. The Ioway boys were approaching the age at which they would normally be learning to hunt and to become warriors. Van Quickenborne reported they "all wept when the hoe was put into their hands for the first time." Another teacher at the school remarked, "it had constantly to be impressed upon the boys that manual labor was not a thing to be ashamed of."

In January 1825, Father Van Quickenborne reported that several Ioway leaders returned to St. Louis for a meeting with William Clark. During their stay in the city, several of the Ioway students traveled into the city to visit the headmen. The boys "were well dressed and behaved extremely well." Van Quickenborne wrote later, "On entering the city one of them drove the cart in which the others were [riding], which amazed the Indian fathers exceedingly. They were highly satisfied and General Clark, I have been told, said after the talk was over, to the Agent: 'I wish all the Indian boys were with Catholics.'"

❋   ❋   ❋

By 1826, Clark and his superiors in the War Department in Washington, D.C., were advocating a general policy of removal and assimilation for all the Indian nations living in and around the state of Missouri. They believed that if native people were to survive in the new nation, they would have to learn to live in the manner of their white neighbors. In a letter to Secretary of War James Barbour in March 1826, Clark outlined several steps that he believed would help native people become self-sufficient.

Perhaps foremost in Clark's plan for reform was an initiative that called for Indian agents to meet systematically with all Indian nations holding land claims inside U.S. territories and states and convince them to relinquish those claims. In return, the U.S. government would reserve suitable parcels of land west of the Missouri River on which members of these nations could live, safely removed from the possibility of conflict with white settlers and members of other tribes. Clark reasoned that once they settled on these reservations, Indian people would finally be free from a life of constant movement and warfare and could focus on learning to read and write, as well as acquiring practical skills in weaving, blacksmithing, and European-American methods of farming.

Clark had always believed agriculture could play a critical role in the government's effort to help native people become self-sufficient because it could provide the means by which they could feed themselves. He disapproved of traditional native forms of communal farming, which the tribes had successfully employed for centuries, because he felt it stifled the spirit of competition and private enterprise. As an alternative to the tradition of common fields, he suggested that native farmers be encouraged to own their fields individually. Clark's hope was that private ownership would allow farmers to reap the benefits of their own efforts and encourage them to work harder to improve their crop yields for their own profit. "Property alone," wrote Clark, " . . . can keep up pride of an Indian and make him ashamed of his drunkenness, begging, lying, and stealing."

Clark also believed it was important that the U.S. government encourage the Indian nations to alter their traditional form of government from one based on hereditary leadership to one in which leaders were elected by popular vote. He thought that a civil government would help to unify tribes like the Ioway that had scattered into various bands, each led by a different headman. He hoped that an elected government would also make life within tribes more peaceful. "It is believed," Clark wrote to Secretary of War Barbour, "that executive agents of this authority will prevent Indians from killing one another for the Chief place, and keep the inferior officers . . . within the bounds of their duty."

In conclusion, Clark reminded the secretary that if these reforms proved successful, the government would no longer need to support Indian nations with annuities. This, he wrote, would allow the United States to "free the treasury from what would otherwise remain an ever lasting charge upon it."

It was to achieve this vision of Indian reform among the Ioway that Thomas McKenney had assigned Colonel Martin Palmer to become the Ioways' first subagent in March 1825. Palmer had first encountered the Ioway as a member of Henry Atkinson's Missouri expedition of 1819. Since that time, he had served as a member of both the Missouri territorial and state legislature, where his aggressive personality had earned him the nickname "the ring-tailed panther." Palmer's tenure as subagent to the Ioway ended quickly, however. After serving in the position for only five months, Palmer left for Texas, where he joined the struggle to help Texas gain its independence from Mexico. In his letter of resignation, he complained, "I can not speak [the Ioway] language and I wood [sic] be of no use to the government." Few employees of the War Department appeared eager to become Palmer's replacement. One subsequent appointee to the post died soon after taking the job, and a second refused to accept the assignment at all.

John Dougherty replaced Benjamin O'Fallon as Indian agent

of the upper Missouri River in 1827. A native of Kentucky and son of a Revolutionary War veteran, Dougherty had first traveled west at age seventeen to work for trader Manuel Lisa. Both he and his brother Henry had been part of the Missouri expedition, where John had served as O'Fallon's interpreter and assistant. Dougherty met with White Cloud to discuss the high turnover of the Ioways' Indian subagents, which the headman believed was the cause of "much evil" among the tribe. According to White Cloud, this evil showed itself in the fact that the tribe's young men had been spending too much time fighting with other tribes and too little time engaged in hunting and in learning how to farm.

White Cloud believed that the situation was so confusing that the Ioway "Chiefs, Braves, and young men have become like a herd of elk being separately shot at in thick timber, but [continue to] run round and round in the same place confused, lost and bewildered, and capable of doing nothing until they are all shot down." In an effort to solve the problem Dougherty appointed Andrew S. Hughes, a fellow Kentucky native, to be the Ioways' subagent in 1828, though he had once reported that Hughes had a "very slender means of making himself respectable as a public agent among the Indians." Despite Dougherty's misgivings and the rocky relationship between the two men, Hughes held the post for nearly a decade and in doing so, helped give the new Ioway Agency at least some stability.

The Treaty of 1824 had required the Ioway to leave Missouri by 1826. The War Department established the Ioway Agency as the new home for the displaced tribe. Defined as the land that lay along Missouri's western border at the Missouri River, the Platte country, which now includes the Missouri counties of Platte, Buchanan, Andrew, Holt, Atchison, and Nodaway, was designated as Indian Territory and, as such, was off-limits to white settlers. The Ioway shared the agency with the Missouri River branch of the Sac and Fox. Led by Quashquame, the Sac and Fox of the Missouri consisted of pro-American members of the two tribes that had migrated away from the Mississippi

River valley during the War of 1812. Many had lived in the Platte country since the war's end. Those Indians who elected to live near the agency established camps in Buchanan County, Missouri, about one mile west of the Platte River along the Big Pigeon and Little Pigeon Creeks.

Immediately after moving the Ioway and the Sac and Fox to the agency, John Dougherty became alarmed over the region's inability to support the agency's population. Just days after assuming his duties as the Indian agent of the upper Missouri, he worried openly to Secretary of War Barbour about the dwindling supply of game in the Platte River country and the effect it was having on the tribes' ability to sustain themselves. "The game in the Indian Country lying to the [West South West], etc. of the state of Missouri for a distance of [400] to 800 miles is nearly exhausted so much so that the tribes who inhabit it, starve at least one half of the time not withstanding all the rations they receive [from the] Government at the different military posts." He warned the secretary that without annuities and their blacksmith "it will be impossible for [the Indians] to live, for as I before stated their country is so barren and destitute of game they cannot procure [a] sufficiency of Peltries, and wealth to more than half clothe and feed themselves."

On another occasion, Dougherty warned William Clark, "As the game is exhausted in the vicinity of [the] villages [of the Omaha, Otoe, Missouria, and Ioway] . . . I cannot see how those poor wretches who inhabit it can live long unless our government should lend a hand in teaching them to till the soil."

Agent Hughes believed that the Ioway living at his agency were making great strides in learning to farm like white farmers. "The White Cloud's band [has] received all the instructions that I deem necessary for them to receive," he reported to Clark in November 1829. "They have raised plenty of corn and other vegetables and will have considerable of a surplus. The women can spin and weave." Just two months later, however, Dougherty painted a far less optimistic portrait of the Ioways' progress:

[The Indians] have made no advance . . . of agriculture [they know] nothing more than they have perhaps always known . . . to raise in a very rude manner, a little corn, a few beans and pumpkins; and even this confined to a very few, out of the numerous tribes on the Missouri; and as to "education," there is not a single Indian man, woman, or child, to my knowledge, from the head of the Missouri to the mouth of the Kansas river, that knows one letter from another. . . .

[As to] the "conditions" of the Indians in Missouri [agency] generally, I can only say that the Kanzas, Iowas, Ottoes, and the Yancton [sic] band of the Sioux, from the diminution and scarcity of game in this country, [will] starve at least half the year, and are very badly clad.

Clark's vision of a "civilized" and "reformed" Ioway tribe seemed to be progressing slowly, if at all. Lifting the tribe out of poverty proved to be far more difficult than either William Clark or the U.S. War Department had expected. Similarly, the dream of a life on the agency that was free from violence proved to be equally elusive. Like the Ioway, all of the tribes living in the lower Missouri River valley were poor and hungry. Their poverty was made worse by the fact that most of the tribes were increasingly confined in their movements by land treaties and by other equally desperate neighboring tribes. Members of some of the tribes reacted violently to the desperate conditions in which they found themselves.

7

Struggle for Survival

By the end of the 1820s, the Ioway tribe faced two critical challenges: the loss of their land, and deepening poverty. The Ioway people needed access to an adequate amount of land and resources in order to sustain themselves. Without enough land for hunting, they grew weak and hungry. Weakness, in turn, made them less able to protect the small amount of land they had from the advances of larger and stronger rival tribes.

John Dougherty reported in January 1828 that the aggressive Sac and Fox, led by Keokuk, were attempting to run the Ioway and Otoe out of a small piece of prime hunting ground near the mouth of the Nodaway River, just north of present-day St. Joseph, Missouri. "I have no doubt," warned Dougherty, "of its being the intention of these crafty [Sac and Fox] to continue crowding the Otoes and Ioways until they . . . get possession of [that] country to which they certainly have no claim whatever." Such increasing pressure from the surrounding tribes forced the Ioway to travel longer distances to obtain food. That same year an Ioway headman named Little Star led a desperate hunting party far up the Boyer River, almost to the present-day

A Kentuckian by birth, John Dougherty accompanied Stephen Long on the Missouri expedition as an interpreter in 1819 and replaced Benjamin O'Fallon as Indian agent of the upper Missouri River in 1827. As an Indian agent, Dougherty oversaw the Ioway subagency, located at present-day Agency, Missouri, and supervised the Ioway's subagent, Andrew S. Hughes. After being forced out of his job for political reasons in 1837, Dougherty remained in Clay County, Missouri, where he was elected to the Missouri legislature. (Courtesy of the State Historical Society of Missouri, Columbia.)

Minnesota state line, to hunt for food on land controlled by their rivals the Dakota.

In an attempt to ease intertribal tensions over land, Dougherty called a council with the Omaha, Otoe, Kansas, Pawnee, Sac and Fox, Shawnee, and Ioway in June 1828 at the newly established Fort Leavenworth. In his report to William Clark, the agent admitted that lasting peace was "very uncertain between all nations." Nonetheless, he optimistically predicted that the treaty of peace and friendship agreed to by the nations participating in the council would "be of some considerable duration." Dougherty continued, "I never saw so much good feeling and apparent good faith among Indian tribes some of whom never knew of peace between themselves before."

For the most part, the treaty Dougherty drafted resembled others signed by the Ioway over the previous years. The agreement called for the participating nations to end all hostilities among themselves. It prohibited them from attempting to resolve any future intertribal conflicts without Dougherty's direct oversight. The fifth article of the treaty, however, ordered the tribes to "agree to take by the hand" and accept the presence of any Indian nations the federal government chose to resettle in their vicinity. In other words, the Ioway and their neighbors who occupied the already crowded Missouri River valley were expected to live together in peace, even as the government moved other uprooted tribes into the region.

This treaty clause reflected the government's continued interest in using Indian removal as a tool to end the violence between dispossessed natives and land-hungry settlers. With the passage of the Indian Removal Act in 1830, the federal government formalized the resettlement program they had employed for years. By moving eastern tribes such as the Potawatomi, Shawnee, Delaware, Piankashaw, Wea, Seneca, Quapaw, and Cherokee west of the Mississippi River, the government greatly increased the stress on tribes then living in Missouri.

As the population of Indians forced to move west grew, so did the number of whites who lived on Missouri's western border. Dougherty and Hughes spent much of their time over the next few years trying to keep settlers and Indians on their respective sides of the one-hundred-mile-long boundary line that separated the state of Missouri from the Platte country and in dealing with the violence that sometimes resulted when the two populations collided.

As early as 1824 the Missouri General Assembly had passed a law that was intended to keep settlers and Indians from crossing the border. Officially titled "An Act to Restrain Intercourse with Indians within the State," the law forbade anyone to invite Indians into Missouri for the purpose of trade. It also made it illegal for anyone to have business dealings with Indians in any location. While the law provided some exceptions for licensed fur traders, it specifically prohibited settlers from supplying native people on either side of the state line with liquor.

Not to be stopped by the state's attempts to control their movements, some desperately hungry Ioway continued to conduct raids on traders and settlers living inside Missouri. Agent Hughes fielded a number of complaints and demands for compensation from outraged citizens who claimed the Ioway had threatened their families, damaged their property, stolen horses, and killed hogs. Ioway raiders also harassed traders, whose merchandise made them an irresistible target. On at least one occasion in 1830 some Ioway men broke into an American Fur Company warehouse at the site of present-day St. Joseph to steal deer hides. Other Ioway robbed numerous traders traveling on the Missouri River.

Missouri residents and businessmen felt violated by Ioway raids into their state, and the Ioway felt equally violated when settlers stole property and trespassed on Indian land. A band of whites crossed into the Platte country from Missouri and stole horses and several other items from White Cloud and his family in the winter of 1829. Raids like these, coupled with the increased number of squatters illegally building homesteads inside the Platte country, only increased the Ioways' level of hostility towards whites.

In the summer of 1829, the Ioways' outrage over the white people's aggressive push onto their land turned violent near Missouri's northern border. In late June, Great Walker, who by that time was known as Big Neck, and members of his band of Ioway camped near the homes of some settlers along the Chariton River in what is now Adair County, Missouri. During a visit to the home of James Myers, an argument occurred between some of the Ioway and members of the Myers family. Some accounts reported that the disagreement started after the settlers gave the Ioway a large amount of liquor and then robbed them. Others stated that the Ioways' demands for food, clothing, and horses started the fight. The argument worsened, then ended after the Ioway killed some of the family's livestock. The natives reportedly told the settlers that they had no right to be on Ioway land and threatened to kill them if they did not leave.

Fearful that the Ioway would return to attack, the settlers asked citizens from nearby Howard County to help mount a defense. In response, twenty-six men arrived at the settlement in mid-July and proceeded to follow Big Neck's trail north along the Chariton River until they found his camp. When the party approached the camp, a gun battle erupted in which at least seven of the white men were shot. Myers's father, John, died immediately and two other men, James Winn and Powell Owenby, were wounded in the battle and killed by the Ioway after the settlers retreated. Four wounded men were able to return to the settlement. One of them, Fields Trammel, died later of his wounds. An Ioway man known as Ioway Jim later alleged that an Ioway baby was shot and that Big Neck lost both a brother and a sister in the battle.

As the surviving settlers and their families fled to Howard County, word of the battle spread quickly across the region. Andrew Hughes immediately led a search for Big Neck and his followers. As an expression of remorse and cooperation, White Cloud, who was not involved in the incident, agreed to travel to Jefferson Barracks with General Henry Leavenworth to be held, along with a group of Sac and Fox and Missouria Indians, as collateral until Big Neck could be apprehended. Agent Hughes traveled more than two thousand miles before finally catching up with Big Neck and seventy men, women, and children north of the Missouri border.

The following spring, Big Neck and at least four other Ioway stood trial for murder in Huntsville, Missouri. The court found them not guilty, in part because it judged that, even though the incident took place eighteen miles inside the state of Missouri in what is now Schuyler County, the Ioway believed they were on their own land north of the Missouri border at the time of the incident. Perhaps more important, the court found that the whites had started the confrontation by following the Ioway to their camp. Even after the trial, Big Neck continued to defy the land cession he agreed to in the Treaty of 1824. He spent the remainder of his life outside the Ioway Agency.

After the Big Neck incident, the U.S. Government increased its efforts to establish boundaries between the tribes living between the Mississippi and Missouri Rivers. In July 1830, William Clark—this time working with Colonel Willoughby Morgan, commander of Fort Crawford—called a peace council near the fort at Prairie du Chien with members of the Sac and Fox, Ioway, Otoe-Missouria, Wahpekute Dakota, Yankton Dakota, and Santee Dakota nations. Clark's first objective was to settle the land disputes in what is now western Iowa and southwest Minnesota that the treaty of 1825 had failed to resolve. However, Clark intended to push the matter one step further by convincing the tribes that ceding the land in question to the United States was the best way to forge an everlasting peace.

In the council, the Ioway delegation expressed their support for Clark's efforts. As he stood face to face with more than one hundred of his allies and enemies on the council grounds, White Cloud boldly voiced his support of the United States. As he stood before the gathering with his war club at his side, this veteran of eighteen battles delivered a message of peace and reconciliation, not of war.

As White Cloud addressed those in the delegation whom he considered to be the enemies of his people—the Sac and Fox headmen Keokuk and Wapello and the Dakota leader Wabasha—the official council secretary, John Ruland, wrote down his words. "Look upon me," the Ioway leader declared, "and you look upon almost a white man." White Cloud proceeded to scold his foes for breaking a peace treaty they had made on that same council ground five years earlier. He criticized them for the violent attacks they had conducted against white settlers and against his own people and openly doubted their willingness to end their brutality. Waving his war club, he said sarcastically, "All [the] people you see here, who wear one of these things think themselves very great."

White Cloud then directed his comments toward those he regarded as his friends—William Clark, Andrew Hughes, and the U.S. military delegation. Reminding Clark of his continued support of government efforts to "civilize" the tribes living in and around the state of Missouri, White Cloud proudly reported, "I have succeeded pretty well in following your advice . . . I have learned to plough and now I eat my own bread, and it makes me large and strong . . . I follow your advice in everything . . . Even my children are at work making cloth."

White Cloud then turned his attention once more to his enemies. "These people eat everything," he teased, "and yet are lean. They can't get fat even by eating their own words." He challenged his enemies to abandon the path of war and to join him in adopting the ways of the white people. Once again brandishing his war club, he concluded, "When I was young, I used to pride myself in one of these things, but now I mean to throw it aside. I know of other things."

White Cloud's speech outlined the only path he believed would ensure the long-term survival of his poverty-stricken people. He had recalled his own days as a young warrior who had once killed white men. In those days, when Europeans and Americans did not outnumber native people, he had thought it was possible to resist them. White Cloud now understood that it was no longer possible for the Ioway to live the traditional life they had once enjoyed on the open prairies. They had become heavily dependent on the annuities, trade goods, and U.S. military protection for their very survival. Seeing no other option open to him, White Cloud chose to embrace the life of the white people.

The Ioway leader Crane echoed White Cloud's words when he spoke later to the council. "I can only say as you do." He told Clark and Morgan, "I want peace with every body." Crane also expressed support for the concept of selling Ioway land. "I don't think 'tis fear of us that induces [the federal government] to buy our lands," he told the delegation, "but 'tis for our peace and comfort. I hope all the Red Skins here are as well satisfied as I and my people. We only wish to have an equal portion with the [other tribes]." After the signing, however, the Ioway claimed that, because the government had not supplied them with an interpreter, they did not fully understand the amount of land they had agreed to sell. White Cloud, Crane, and eight other Ioway leaders had, apparently unknowingly, signed away all of their land between the Des Moines River and the Missouri River in exchange for ten annual payments of twenty-five hundred dollars.

Though the Sac and Fox also signed the Treaty of 1830, their chief negotiator had been Keokuk, a rival of Black Hawk's. Black Hawk had chosen to avoid the council and to ignore the treaty. Trouble developed the next year when he and his followers refused to be moved west of the Mississippi River, as the treaty had stipulated. Black Hawk's resistance and the resulting buildup of eighteen hundred American militiamen along the Mississippi fueled tensions that reached all the way to the Ioway Agency. Agent Hughes was especially concerned about Black Hawk's movements because of the Missouri River band of the Sac and Fox that lived near his agency.

In June 1831, Hughes stated that he believed Black Hawk had crossed the Mississippi River into present-day Iowa. He worried that the Sac and Fox leader and some of his allies had traveled west from Illinois to hide with their kinsmen at the Ioway Agency in the Platte country. Joshua Pilcher, the Sac and Fox agent on the Mississippi River, doubted Hughes's information and complained about it in a letter to William Clark. He reported to Clark that Hughes's claim had "thrown the whole frontier into commotion [and] driven off the [white] inhabitants." Pilcher admitted that his information was no more reliable and wrote that "the country is filled with so many idle rumors, that [the] whole of my time would be occupied in writing were I to undertake to communicate them."

According to one rumor, Black Hawk's Sac and Fox party planned to attack and rob the Omaha Indians of the annuities they had just received at Fort Leavenworth. The Ioway sent a messenger to warn the Omaha of the threat. As they transported their provisions to their agency, the Omaha altered their route of return to avoid the supposed Sac and Fox war party. As they made their way up the west side of the Missouri River, the Omaha stumbled on a small group of Ioway. Perhaps because the Omaha mistakenly believed the Ioway to be members of the rumored Sac and Fox raiding party, a skirmish broke out in which the Omaha killed Crane's son.

The violent death of Crane's son greatly heightened tensions in the region. While John Dougherty blamed Black Hawk's band of the Sac and Fox for creating the excitement and confusion that led to the killing, he also suspected that the tragedy was committed in retaliation for the Ioway killing of an Omaha boy several months earlier. Andrew Hughes also believed revenge was the motive and claimed the murder of Crane's son would not have happened if Dougherty had arrested the suspect in the earlier murder.

The Ioway immediately demanded justice in the matter. While White Cloud and the other Ioway headmen struggled to keep their young men from attacking the Omaha in revenge, they appealed to agent Hughes and the government to quickly punish the guilty Omaha. The Ioway, Hughes informed Clark, are "looking to the United States for protection," and Hughes warned that if the government failed to deliver justice, there would be "no end to Indian outrage and murder—our treaties . . . [will] become a dead letter."

Reining in his young men proved impossible for White Cloud. The young warriors felt that by refusing to allow them to organize a war party, White Cloud was denying them an important traditional rite of passage by which they would prove their bravery and save their honor. In defiance, nearly one hundred Ioway warriors set out in an unsuccessful retaliatory raid on the Omaha. Agent Hughes wrote to Clark for advice in the matter while Clark, in turn, appealed to Secretary of War Lewis Cass for additional troops to help control this and similar unrest across the Missouri River valley:

> I see no means by which the wars between those Tribes can be prevented but by an effective force of troops authorized to act, and I am inclined to believe that in addition to the Infantry now on our western frontier, [with] *one* or *two* Regiments of mounted men armed and equipped for active service, stationed at such points as to enable them to act with effect, we could be able to repress the reckless spirit of the Indians.

While the controversy surrounding the death of Crane's son simmered, the Ioway suffered another staggering loss. In early September 1831 Big Neck was killed while trying to retrieve stolen property from a band of Dakota. Again, the Ioway chiefs appealed to Hughes and the government to act quickly to arrest and punish the offenders. Hughes worried that the government's failure to do so would leave the Ioway and the Missouri band of the Sac and Fox no choice but to launch a war against the Dakota. "I am well satisfied," Hughes warned, "that it will be a more protracted and bloody contest, than any heretofore witnessed."

In the spring of 1832, panic among settlers in and around the state of Missouri reached a peak as the militia pursued Black Hawk and his followers across northern Illinois and southern Wisconsin. Throughout the conflict, Andrew Hughes continued to worry that Black Hawk or other members of his Sac and Fox band would flee to the Missouri River, bringing violence and bloodshed to the Ioway Agency. Many settlers on the western border of Missouri held similar fears and abandoned their farms for the protection of nearby towns and settlements. To ensure that so-called hostile Sac and Fox Indians did not travel west from Illinois, four companies of U.S. Rangers patrolled the region between the Mississippi and the Missouri Rivers. The tribes along the Missouri River were warned not to hunt in the vicinity of the troops for fear they would be mistaken for Black Hawk sympathizers.

Hughes's level of anxiety reached a near frenzy when Sac and Fox Indians from the Mississippi River region successfully evaded the troops and made their way to the Ioway Agency. Rumors circulated that Black Hawk was also sending warriors farther west to form alliances of war with the Osage and Kansas Indians. Hughes feared that the Mississippi River Sac and Fox were Black Hawk supporters trying to incite the Indians on his agency to rise up in revolt against white settlers. The discovery that a number of young Ioway and Missouri Sac and Fox warriors had disappeared from the agency, allegedly for the purposes of hunting, only intensified his fears that violence was unavoidable.

Pressured to take action by whites living on Missouri's western border, Hughes, with the settlers' help, arrested twenty-two of the Mississippi River Sac and Fox visitors who, he reported, had "made their appearance in questionable shape, with suspicion at their heels." Later, when another group of Ioway and Sac and Fox men arrived at his house demanding to be fed and insulting his wife, Hughes took six of them into custody as well. A clearly shaken Hughes informed Clark that, despite their earlier denials, the headmen at his agency claimed knowledge of a months-old plan to attack settlers near the Missouri River. "They lied to me," Hughes wrote to Clark. "These tribes are in heart and soul with the enemy, and nothing but Annuities restrain them from scalping our people."

The arrival of U.S. troops in late July cooled the situation to the point that Hughes released some of the imprisoned Ioway and the Sac and Fox leaders. Clark assured Hughes that the

Mississippi River Sac and Fox who had appeared at his agency were friendly toward the United States and had traveled to his agency seeking the protection of the government. Clark reasoned that the fear caused by their presence was unfounded since no violent acts had been committed. Upon learning that Hughes had taken Indian prisoners, Clark's tone became harsher. "I regret very much you have taken those hostages as I cannot perceive any necessity for doing so nor for the alarm which appears to have been felt by the inhabitants on their account." Missouri Governor John Miller openly worried that Hughes's actions would cause more of Black Hawk's Sac and Fox to leave the Mississippi River to come to the Ioway Agency out of concern for their captive kinsmen. The tense situation did not end until settlers along Missouri's western border received word of Black Hawk's defeat and capture in August of 1832.

As the uncertainty surrounding the whereabouts of Black Hawk drew to a close, several Ioway leaders had the chance to have their portraits painted by the artist George Catlin as he passed through the Platte country. A native of Pennsylvania, Catlin had abandoned a career in law a decade earlier to follow his passion for art. By 1830 he had moved to St. Louis to specialize in painting portraits of American Indians. Catlin left St. Louis on the steamboat *Yellowstone* in March 1832 to begin an eighteen-hundred-mile journey on the Missouri River. During that trip he created 135 paintings, many of which turned out to be the best of his long career. As he visited the Ioway, he noted that they were "the farthest departed from primitive modes" of all the tribes in the region. "They are depending chiefly on their cornfields for their substance," he reported, "though their appearance, both in their dwellings and personal looks . . . is that of the primitive Indian."

Catlin's paintings and writings show that he was fascinated by the Ioways' "primitive" looks. In his *Letters and Notes on the North American Indians,* he boasted that his portraits of the warriors Shooting Cedar and Busy Man captured them tastefully dressed and equipped, the one with his war club on his arm, the other with bow and arrows in his hand; both wear around their waist beautiful buffalo robes and both had turbans of vari-colored cotton shawls, purchased of the Fur Traders. Around their necks were necklaces of the bear's claws, and a profusion of beads and wampum. Their ears were profusely strung with beads; their naked shoulders curiously streaked and daubed with red paint.

Catlin's fascination with the Ioway lasted long after he left them to continue his journey up the Missouri River. In 1844 he led a group of more than a dozen Ioway people, including White Cloud's son Francis, to London where they appeared in a traveling show.

By April 1833, the Ioway were increasingly unsatisfied with the government's failure to deliver justice in the case of the Omaha killing of Crane's son two years earlier. To avenge the murder, twelve Ioway men formed a war party and traveled up the Missouri River to attack the Omaha near John Dougherty's agency at Bellevue, near present-day Omaha, Nebraska. The party succeeded in killing six Omaha men and in taking a woman and a child hostage. Agent Dougherty worked quickly to prevent the Omaha from retaliating by sending the much-revered Omaha leader Big Elk to the Ioway Agency to discuss the issue with White Cloud and the other Ioway headmen.

As he had in previous cases of intertribal violence, White Cloud felt it was the responsibility of the U.S. government, not of the Omaha, to bring justice to the Ioway who had committed the murders. He assisted agent Hughes in the capture of eight of the Ioway believed responsible for murdering the Omaha. Hughes turned the individuals over to Major Bennett Riley, who transported them to Fort Leavenworth for trial. While in Leavenworth, one of the imprisoned Ioway vowed to kill White Cloud for assisting in his capture. In 1834, after making his escape from the fort, the man who had threatened the headman raised a party to track him down. Following White Cloud up the Nodaway River, the party caught and killed him in the vicinity of present-day Montgomery County, Iowa.

After the murder, one of the members of the party that killed White Cloud took refuge among the Otoe-Missouria, who killed him upon discovering his crime. Another of the killers returned to White Cloud's village where White Cloud's son, Francis White Cloud, confronted him. The younger White Cloud avenged his father's death by killing the man's dogs and horses and destroying his lodge. Francis White Cloud stopped short of killing the man, however, telling him, "You have killed the greatest man who ever made a moccasin track on the Nodaway; you must, therefore, be yourself a great man, since the Great Spirit gave you the victory. To call you a dog would make my father less than a dog." Even after a council of Ioway headmen asked Francis White Cloud to kill the man in revenge for the headman's death, he again refused, saying, "I cannot kill so brave a man." The Ioway finally punished White Cloud's murderer by assigning another headman to kill him.

Like his father, Francis White Cloud was pushed into the role of headman at a young age. Just twenty-four and undecorated in battle when his father died, the young man at first refused his position of leadership. That October, when agent Hughes submitted a report outlining the receipt of annuities by the Ioway and the Sac and Fox under his charge, he reported that Francis White Cloud had given his uncle, No Heart, the honor of accepting the tribe's annuities. This honor meant that the younger White Cloud wanted No Heart to take his place as headman of the Ioway. After a time, the young warrior was persuaded to take his rightful place, alongside No Heart, at the council of headmen where he followed the policies favored by his father. "One of my sisters and other young [women] have been taught to spin and weave," Francis White Cloud told the council. "My father approved this and encouraged it. He also taught the lessons of peace, and counseled me not to go to war, except in my own defense. I have made up my mind to listen always to that talk." No Heart, though far more experienced in battle than Francis White Cloud, also supported the tribe's efforts to work peacefully with the United States. Together, the two led the Ioway for several years, encouraging them to adopt the ways of their white neighbors.

In death, White Cloud quickly achieved the status of a martyr and became a mythic figure in the eyes of native and nonnative people alike. On the one hand, some mourned him as the last of a generation of Ioway leaders who remembered a time when the tribe still lived according to its traditional ways. While White Cloud had been forced by the white establishment to abandon his native lifestyle, he ironically became a symbol of the virtues of that lifestyle after his death.

On the other hand, many settlers and government officials remembered White Cloud as a faithful "friend of the white man." As a young warrior he had fought in eighteen battles and had been responsible for the death of two French traders. The fact that in later life White Cloud had laid down his weapons and given in to the demands of the United States gave government officials hope that Indian people could be "civilized."

As they grieved over the loss of White Cloud, the Ioway were forced to contend with the growing problem of American settlers squatting on their land. During his visit to the region the year before White Cloud's death, the German Prince Maximilian von Wied noted that settlers lived as much as "fifteen or sixteen miles within the Indian Territory." In some places in the Platte country, the settlers reportedly lived so close to Ioway villages that their livestock roamed through and destroyed the Indians' meager fields.

By 1835 the problem had become important enough to attract the attention of the Department of Indian Affairs in Washington, D.C. Commissioner Elbert Herring instructed Hughes to warn all squatters living in the Platte country that they must move immediately or risk being forcibly removed by U.S. Mounted Rangers. By July 1835, Hughes reported that he had delivered notices of removal to a total of sixty-four settlers, though he suspected there were many others "skulking and lurking about, who have no particular residences." The following February, Colonel Henry Dodge, the Rangers' commanding officer, again informed settlers that they were in violation of the law and must move. However, because the squatters expected Missouri to annex the Platte country soon, Dodge's warnings had little effect.

At the same time that the military was trying to prevent settlers from moving to the Platte country, Commissioner of Indian Affairs Elbert Herring allowed 252 Potawatomi, who had recently sold their land near Chicago, to temporarily move into the region in December 1835. The group was supposed to resettle in western Iowa with 500 of their fellow tribesmen but chose to live near the Ioway and the Sac and Fox instead. As the U.S. government worked to find a permanent home for the Potawatomi, other bands of the tribe migrated from Indiana and Michigan to join them.

The growing number of Indians moving into the region greatly distressed Missouri politicians, who had coveted the Platte country for years. Members of Missouri's congressional delegation had been interested in annexing the territory since at least 1829. In December of that year, Senator Thomas Hart Benton and Congressman Spencer Pettis had both written to Secretary of War John Eaton asking that the Ioways' title to the land be extinguished. "[The land] is essential to the State of Missouri," declared Benton, "and hardly desirable to the Indians on account of its narrowness." In 1831, the Missouri General Assembly petitioned the U.S. Congress to request that no additional tribes be assigned to the Platte country. With the help of Missouri Senator Lewis Linn, Congress agreed in June 1836 to extend the state's western border to the Missouri River as soon as all Indian rights to the land could be settled.

The Ioway had long shown interest in selling a portion of the Platte River land to the United States. As early as 1828 several Ioway headmen met with Andrew Hughes to propose the sale of the portion of their claim that was located between the Missouri state border and the Platte River. In return, the Ioway leaders asked that money from the sale of the land be applied toward sending their children to white schools to be educated. They also asked that the government set aside a separate piece of land for Ioway mixed-bloods and for any Ioway who received an education in white schools and decided not to live as their native relatives did.

That the Ioway would consider selling their land shows the depth of their poverty. Game populations had decreased so much in the region during the 1820s and early 1830s that the fur trade had bottomed out. Maximilian von Wied described the environmental problems he saw when he traveled through the region in the spring of 1833. In preparation for his trip to America, the German prince had read the glowing descriptions of the lower Missouri River valley's lush green landscapes and abundant game population recorded twenty years earlier by British naturalist John Bradbury. As he traveled west, however, he marveled at the changes that had taken place since Bradbury's time. In his journal Maximilian noted the large-scale clearing of trees in the vicinity of Fort Leavenworth—where one of the main Ioway villages was located—and around the new town of Liberty, Missouri. While deer and wild turkeys could still be found in the vicinity of the Platte River, he wrote that bear and panthers were rare by that time and elk were virtually nonexistent. In more than one of his journal entries, the prince commented that the once-plentiful beaver, on which the lower Missouri River fur trade had been built, had vanished by 1833.

The decrease in game meant that Ioway hunters were finding it difficult to feed their tribe or gather enough hides to trade for the various manufactured goods they had come to depend on for survival. As a result, the Ioway had become so heavily in-debted that the American Fur Company demanded that goods sold to the tribe on credit be paid for out of their annuities. Much of this debt was caused by the Ioways' need for necessities like traps, blankets, guns, ammunition, and cloth. One ledger from the early 1830s indicates that the Ioway collectively owed a single trader by the name of Bushnell more than nine hundred dollars—the equivalent of approximately eighteen thousand in today's dollars—for such items.

Liquor also was the cause of an increasingly large part of the Ioways' trade debt. When he traveled to Council Bluff with the Long expedition in 1819, Edwin James had noted in his journal that he believed the Ioway were among the tribes who were "excessively attached" to alcohol. As fur supplies along the lower Missouri River dwindled, unscrupulous traders found that by exploiting the Ioways' addiction to illegal liquor, they could not only make handsome profits but also take business away from more ethical competitors. One of the Sac and Fox headmen living on the Ioway Agency explained to John Dougherty that traders often cheated and robbed the Indians in these deals. "[Our] young men hunted hard and killed but little, owing to the scarcity of game, and when they succeeded in collecting a few skins, and exchange them for a few goods, the whiskey smugglers come in with their kegs, make us drunk, and bear off everything we possess, and leave us to awaken from our drunken dreams naked and hungry."

By the 1830s, the economic cycle that dominated Ioway life at the time was nothing short of catastrophic. Since they had first established trade relations with the French 150 years earlier, the Ioway had gradually shifted from self-sufficiency to heavy dependency on the market economy and the manufactured goods it brought them. When the animal population dwindled from overhunting, they were not able to produce enough animal pelts to buy the goods they needed to hunt and clothe and feed themselves. As a result, the Ioway ran up large debts with the traders. To pay their mounting debts, they had few choices. They had to turn their annual annuities over to the trading houses to satisfy their shortfall. If their annuities were not large enough to cover the debt, they could elect to sell more of their land to the United States. In the end, the traders got much of the Ioways' money, the United States gained more of the Ioways' land, and the Ioway, left with nothing, remained impoverished.

8

Mayan Jegi Chexi Ke
(This Land Here Is Difficult)

In June 1836, a family of horse-stealing settlers nearly succeeded in starting a war between the Missouri Militia and the
Ioway Indians. George Heatherly, his wife, Jenny, and their four
sons were living in what is now Mercer County, Missouri, when
they learned that an Ioway hunting party was camped near
what is now called the Thompson River. Accompanied by James
Dunbar, Alfred Hawkins, and a man named Thomas, the
Heatherlys succeeded in raiding the Ioway camp and stealing a
number of the hunters' horses. The Ioway chased the thieves
south until they caught up with them near the present-day town
of Chillicothe. There, a confrontation between the two groups
turned violent, and Thomas died in a gun battle. The Ioway
retrieved their horses and the surviving members of the
Heatherly party escaped.

After returning to their home, the Heatherlys and their partners decided to tell local authorities that the Ioway had attacked
them without cause. Fearful that James Dunbar would expose
their lie, the other members of the gang killed him and hid his
body. Word of the incident spread quickly throughout north-

The Ioway headman MáñiXáñe, or Great Walker, greatly regretted cosigning the Treaty of 1824, which included the first cession of Ioway land to the United States. In defiance of the treaty, he and a group of his followers refused to move out of the state of Missouri into the region surrounding the Platte River. In 1829, Great Walker, who was then known as TáseXáñe, or Big Neck, and his band of Ioway were involved in a dispute over land that led to the deaths of three settlers and three Ioway. (Courtesy of the State Historical Society of Missouri, Columbia.)

west Missouri. In response, General A. B. Thompson led a group of militia men from Ray and Carroll Counties directly to the scene of the fight, while Colonel Shubael Allen led more than 150 men from Clay County north along Missouri's western border in an attempt to intercept any Ioway who might try to return to their agency on the Platte River.

THE FIRST DISCUSSION OF THE PLATTE PURCHASE

Walter Ufer's mural painting, *The First Discussion of the Platte Purchase*, incorrectly suggests that Indian agent Andrew Hughes first proposed the Platte Purchase during a militia meeting on the farm of Weakly Dale near Liberty, Missouri, in the summer of 1835. In fact, Missouri Senator Thomas Hart Benton and Congressman Spencer Pettis had asked the secretary of war to "extinguish" the Indians' claim to the land as early as 1829. (Lunette Mural from the Missouri State Capitol, reproduction courtesy of the Missouri State Archives.)

Thompson quickly found the Ioway hunting party and determined that they had acted in self-defense when they killed Thomas. Thompson disbanded the militia and the incident referred to as the "Heatherly War" ended without further violence. In mid-July the Carroll County sheriff apprehended the Heatherlys, who, along with their accomplice Alfred Hawkins, stood trial for the murder of James Dunbar. Only Hawkins was convicted.

In his continuing effort to end this kind of violence, William Clark was eager to separate the Ioway and Missouri Sac and Fox from their white neighbors by moving them to the west side of the Missouri River. Clark believed that the river barrier would remove the Indians from the devastations of liquor and the harassment of whites who were hungry to settle on their land. Once transferred to land of their own, the Ioway and Sac

As the Missouri River valley was overhunted in the 1820s and 1830s, the fur trade bottomed out. Unscrupulous traders soon discovered that they could still make handsome profits and take business away from more ethical competitors by trading illegal liquor to the Indians. (Courtesy of the State Historical Society of Missouri, Columbia.)

and Fox would be able to focus on rebuilding a more prosperous and peaceful existence.

After years of warfare and poverty, at least some Indians on the Ioway Agency shared Clark's hopes. John Dougherty reported that one of the Sac and Fox leaders who lived near the agency complained to him that while "bad white men" robbed them of everything but their corn, their "red neighbors who hate to work" stole even that remaining necessity from them. He told Dougherty that Indians on his agency were too proud to beg and too weak to steal, adding sadly,

We are tired of the land on which we now live. . . . We wish to move, but not in the direction of the Mississippi, we want to travel towards the setting sun, we would like to have that (pointing to the Missouri) rapid muddy stream running between us and the White Settlements, we are at war with no nation white or red, we wish for a home to ourselves in exchange for which we are willing to enter into a treaty with our Great Father and to give up all claim to any unsold lands we may have between the Mississippi and Missouri rivers, or any where else on the face of this earth, we are desirous to live at home, quit hunting, work and raise stock like white men do.

The Ioway headmen must have agreed, because in September 1836 they joined their agent Andrew Hughes and the leaders of the Sac and Fox of the Missouri at Fort Leavenworth for a treaty council with Stephen Watts Kearney, the fort's commander. In what became known as the Platte Purchase agreement, the headmen of both nations ceded all of their rights and claims to the land that now makes up the Missouri counties of Platte, Buchanan, Andrew, Holt, Atchison, and Nodaway. In return, the tribes received seventy-five hundred dollars. The treaty ordered that within a year, the Ioway and the Sac and Fox would be moved to two separate land reserves of two hundred square miles each on the south bank of the Great Nemaha River near the border between present-day Kansas and Nebraska. The government agreed to build five "comfortable houses" for the Ioway and to fence off and prepare two hundred acres of land for cultivation. The treaty further promised that the Ioway would receive tools, 205 head of cattle and hogs, and a year's worth of food rations, as well as the instruction of a schoolmaster, a farmer, and a blacksmith.

On March 28, 1837, President Martin Van Buren issued a proclamation that allowed the state of Missouri to annex the Platte River country. Two months later Hughes reported that approximately 992 Ioway had moved across the river to their new home. About 130 Ioway refused to make the move and instead traveled north along the Tarkio River to establish a

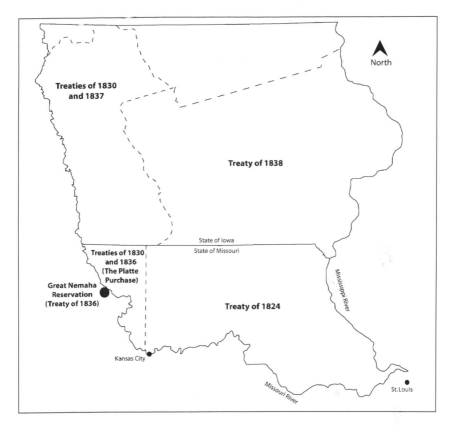

Ioway land cessions, 1824 to 1838. (Map by the author.)

home north of Missouri's northern border, where they would remain until dragoons led by Daniel Boone's son Nathan forced them into Kansas in 1840.

Both Hughes and Kearney expressed concern over the fact that, while a large majority of the Ioway had honorably held up their end of the Platte Purchase treaty, the government had not. They reported that the tribe was in bad need of the supplies and rations it had been promised in the treaty. When the provisions did not arrive, Joseph Robidoux offered to work with the government to provide the tribe with goods on contract. Robidoux was a long-time trader whose trading post, situated along the Missouri River at the foot of the Blacksnake Hills, eventually became the town of St. Joseph, Missouri. His relationship with the Ioway began in the years just after the War of 1812, and he fathered several children with Ioway and Otoe women. One of his daughters, Mary, married Francis White Cloud.

Just three months after settling on the reservation, four Ioway headmen traveled with Hughes to Washington, D.C., to meet once again with a delegation of the Sac and Fox of the Mississippi River led by Keokuk. In Washington, the discussions revolved around the Ioway's long resentment over the treaty of 1830. The Ioway had learned that the Sac and Fox were preparing to cede all of their remaining lands between the Mississippi and the Missouri Rivers to the United States. The Ioway challenged Keokuk's right to sell the land, arguing that it still belonged to the Ioway. In the treaty negotiations the headmen No Heart and Raining each referred to a large map on which the Ioway had drawn the location of all the villages they had lived in between the Missouri River and the Great Lakes over the past two hundred years. They traced their migration from village to village and argued that since many of the lakes and rivers near these villages still had names the Ioway had given them, the land must belong to them. Keokuk admitted that the land had once indeed belonged to the Ioway, but argued that the Sac and Fox owned it because they had forced the Ioway out. "We have always pushed them before us," Keokuk proudly stated. "That is the reason they have marked so many villages on their map."

The Ioway delegation became so angry over the land dispute that they left Washington before the negotiations could be completed. When they reached St. Louis, however, William Clark pressured them into signing a treaty in which they forever gave up their claim to all the lands they had ceded in the 1830 treaty. In return the government would pay them twenty-five hundred dollars' worth of horses and other goods.

Upon their return home some dissatisfied Ioway, unhappy

Like many traders, Joseph Robidoux established favorable economic ties to the Ioway people through marriage. Robidoux's daughter, Mary, married the Ioway leader Francis White Cloud. When the government failed to provide the annuities they promised the Ioway in the 1830s, Robidoux, the founder of the city of St. Joseph, Missouri, provided much-needed supplies to the Ioway on contract. (Courtesy of the State Historical Society of Missouri, Columbia.)

with the way they had been treated in Washington and disappointed with their reservation land, expressed their longing to move back to their ancestral home in the Des Moines River valley. While the Ioway had not occupied the site for nearly a decade and a half, it remained important to them because it held the bones of many of their ancestors and memories of a better life. Perhaps equally attractive to the Ioway was the fact that even though the Platte Purchase agreement confined them to their small reservation in Kansas, they retained legal right to the village sites that were located on the Des Moines River. Denied the supplies and food the government had promised them, and living on land that was already becoming seriously depleted of game, the Ioway considered returning to their former home.

Fearing that the return of the Ioway to the state of Missouri or the Iowa Territory would lead to more confrontations with white settlers, John Dougherty met with five headmen on the reservation and successfully convinced them to sign one final land treaty by which the Ioway gave up their rights to the old village sites. On October 13, 1838, thirteen Ioway headmen, led by Francis White Cloud and No Heart, signed the Treaty of 1838, which ended the tribe's right to claim any land between the Missouri and Mississippi Rivers in exchange for $157,500, the interest from which was to be paid to the tribe annually. That same year, the Missouri General Assembly passed a law prohibiting Indian people of any nation from entering the state without the permission of an Indian agent. For all practical purposes, the Ioway nation's presence inside the state that bore the name of their close relatives the Missouria had come to an end.

By 1838, the lives of the Ioway resembled those of their white neighbors in many ways. Some Ioway grew crops in small private plots, received at least some income through annuities, and, like Francis White Cloud, lived in log homes. The tribe would soon have a school and a teacher, and would receive guidance from a Presbyterian missionary.

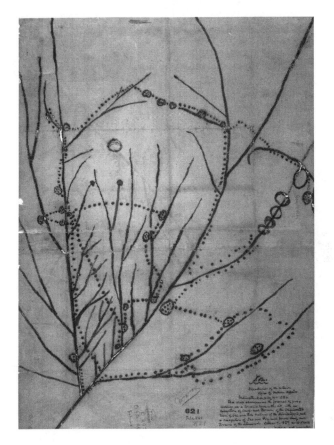

Map of the Missouri, Mississippi, and Illinois River basins, showing the historical settlements of the Ioway Indians, 1837. In 1836, the Ioway Indians learned that the Sac and Fox had recently agreed to sell 1,250,000 acres of land to the United States. The Ioway claimed that they, not the Sac and Fox, owned much of this land. In October 1837 representatives of the Ioway met in Washington, D.C., with Indian Commissioner C. A. Harris and a delegation of Sac and Fox led by Keokuk. The Ioway leader, Na'hjeNing'e, or No Heart, produced this map to document that the Ioway had lived on the disputed land for the previous two centuries. The U.S. government agreed that the Ioway might hold a legal claim to a huge section of land between the Des Moines and Missouri Rivers, in what is now western Iowa. A month later in St. Louis the Ioway relinquished their final rights to the land for twenty-five hundred dollars' worth of horses, goods, and presents. (Courtesy of the National Archives and Records Administration.)

Like his father, White Cloud, Francis White Cloud tried to help his people adjust to the dramatic economic and cultural challenges of living under the domination of the *Ma'unke*, or white people. When the Ioway moved to the Great Nemaha Reservation in 1837, the younger White Cloud encouraged them to become active in farming, weaving, and other manual arts that he hoped would lead them toward self-sufficiency. A decade later, he led a small group of Ioway to Europe, where they performed throughout England and the continent as part of a tour of the painter George Catlin's portrait gallery of Indians. (Courtesy of the State Historical Society of Missouri, Columbia.)

But many Ioway apparently still longed for the old ways. The tribe occupied a ten-by-twenty-mile plot of land to which they had no ancestral connection. Animals like the buffalo, bear, beaver, and elk that had once served as both cultural touchstones and sources of life for the Ioway were either gone, or greatly reduced in number. Many Ioway became keenly aware of the void left by the loss of their traditional homeland and their animal relatives.

The Ioway sometimes left the confines of their small Kansas reservation to engage in many of the traditional activities that had connected them to the earth, the sky, and the animals. But even when they traveled to hunt, hold councils, or go to war, they could not help noticing that the countryside was altered. The land on which they had once hunted and lived and that still held the bones of their ancestors had become the home of the foreign *Ma'unke*, who had reshaped it with their roads, their square houses, and their towns laid out in a grid. There was simply no room left in their homeland for the Ioway to practice anything resembling their traditional lives.

Mahaska, by Sherry Edmundson Fry, 1908. In 1905 retired banker and real estate magnate James Edmundson commissioned sculptor Sherry Fry to create a memorial to his father, William Edmundson, the first white settler in Mahaska County, Iowa. Fry chose the Ioway leader and county namesake Mahaska, better known as White Cloud, as the subject of his sculpture. His richly detailed bronze, which still stands in the courthouse square in Oskaloosa, Iowa, portrays White Cloud as a romanticized "noble savage." (Photograph by the author.)

Epilogue

Survival and Renewal

This book examines a tragic but brief period in the long history of the Ioway people. While the story may give readers the impression that the Ioway and their culture disappeared in the mid–nineteenth century, this is far from being the case. Despite the numerous dramatic setbacks and serious challenges they faced between 1800 and 1838, the Ioway persevered, continuing to change and adapt to the constantly evolving world around them. As the twenty-first century begins, the Ioway not only survive; they are experiencing a renewal of economic and cultural strength.

The Ioway tribe now lives in two separate locations. In the 1880s a portion of the tribe moved from the Great Nemaha Reservation to live in the state of Oklahoma, which was then known as the Indian Territory. This group is officially called the Iowa Tribe of Oklahoma. In 1995, the tribal roll listed 366 people. Today, the tribe owns about six hundred acres of land on which they raise buffalo, cattle, and row crops. It operates a casino, a convenience store, and a tobacco shop near the town of Perkins. BKJ Solutions, a tribally owned company, provides trucking, construction, energy, and environmental services.

Like the Ioway remaining in Kansas and Nebraska, the Iowa Tribe of Oklahoma is also actively involved in preserving its traditional culture. Through their historic preservation program members of the tribe are working to protect traditional knowledge, religion, songs, dances, and language. The tribe has recently opened an aviary where they care for injured eagles. After the passage of the federal Native American Graves Protection and Repatriation Act (NAGPRA) in 1991, they established a preservation office in Princeton, Missouri, and began reclaiming cultural artifacts and ancestral remains that were housed in private museums and government institutions across the country.

Currently, about four hundred Ioway tribal members still live in the area surrounding their original reservation along the banks of the Great Nemaha River in Kansas and Nebraska. The Ioway Tribe of Kansas and Nebraska has a total enrollment of nearly three thousand people. The "northern" Ioway, as they are sometimes called, operate a casino, restaurant, tourist cabins, convenience store, and gas station just west of the town of White Cloud, Kansas. The tribe uses about one third of its land to grow row crops and has dedicated additional acreage for raising cattle.

With the help of NAGPRA, the Ioway Tribe of Kansas and Nebraska has also retrieved artifacts related to its cultural heritage. The tribal complex contains a display of items related to Ioway history, and the tribe has restored the house of a descendant of the first White Cloud, former chief James White Cloud, who lived from 1848 to 1940. The Kansas State Historical Society operates the Native American Heritage Museum ten miles south of the reservation, near the town of Highland. Housed in a former Indian mission boarding school, the museum features exhibits about Ioway history and displays artwork made by tribal members.

For More Reading

One of the best sources for history and information on the Ioway people is Lance M. Foster's excellent Web site, Ioway Cultural Institute, http://ioway.nativeweb.org/. Foster, an enrolled member of the tribe who has written several articles about the Ioway, has collected treaty documents, pictures, articles, bibliographies, and genealogy information and made them easily available online. Linguist and historian Jimm GoodTracks has collected traditional Ioway stories and information about the Ioway language on his Ioway-Otoe-Missouria Language Web site, http://iowayotoelang.nativeweb.org/. For a general overview of Ioway history and culture as well as interviews with several tribal members, see the 2007 documentary *Lost Nation: The Ioway*, available on DVD from Fourth Wall Films, http://www.iowaymovie.com/.

Among published sources, Lynn M. Alex's *Iowa's Archaeological Past* (Iowa City: University of Iowa Press, 1980; revised and expanded, 2000) provides an excellent introduction to the material culture of the Oneota and their descendants, the Ioway. Researchers interested in the early history of the Ioway should also refer to the work of pioneering archaeologist Mildred Mott Wedel.

First published in 1979 and updated in 1995, Martha Royce Blaine's *The Ioway Indians* (Norman: University of Oklahoma Press) remains the definitive written history of the Ioway. Another good source of information about the early history of the Ioway is Zachary Gussow's *Sac and Fox and Iowa Indians,* vol. 1 (New York: Garland Publishing, 1974). While it does not deal exclusively with the Ioway, Tanis C. Thorne's *The Many Hands of My Relations: French and Indians on the Lower Missouri* (Columbia: University of Missouri Press, 1996) provides a good explanation of the effects of the fur trade on the Indian nations that lived along the lower Missouri River in the eighteenth and nineteenth centuries. Dorothy J. Caldwell's "The Big Neck Affair: Tragedy and Farce on the Missouri Frontier," in the July 1970 edition of the *Missouri Historical Review,* provides the most detailed account of the Ioway leader's 1829 battle with white settlers.

Many of the quotes in this book came from unpublished letters, transcripts, reports, and other documents. One valuable source for such documents is the collection of Ioway Agency files housed at the National Archives. Another resource that I found especially helpful was a book of letters written between 1826 and 1829 by Indian agent John Dougherty. This letter book is housed at the Western Historical Manuscript Collection–Columbia.

Though long out of print, there are several good accounts of the Ioway in early nineteenth-century journals written by European travelers who visited them. Duke Paul (Paul Wilhelm, Duke of Wuerttemberg) discussed the Ioway in detail in his *Travels in the Interior of North America: 1822–1823* (Norman: University of Oklahoma Press, 1973). Several men connected to Stephen H. Long's 1819 Missouri River expedition kept journals of the event that provide accounts of the Ioway. The most complete is Edwin James's "Account of S. H. Long's Expedition, 1819–1820," found in volume 14 of Ruben Gold Thwaites's *Early Western Travels 1748–1846* (Cleveland: Arthur H. Clark Company,

1905). David Meriwether's *My Life in the Mountains and on the Plains* (edited by Robert A. Griffen, Norman: University of Oklahoma Press, 1965) is another valuable account of that expedition and of the Ioway headman White Cloud. George Catlin, who painted portraits of many Ioway in the 1830s and 1840s, wrote briefly about his 1832 visit to the Ioway Agency in his *Letters and Notes on the North American Indians* (reprinted in 1995 by JG Press of North Dighton, Massachusetts). Thomas McKenney and James Hall had the opportunity to interview some of the Ioway leaders mentioned in this book. Their biographies of White Cloud, Great Walker, No Heart, and others appear along with etchings of Charles Bird King's portraits in *History of the Indian Tribes of North America.* McKenney and Hall's history, first published in 1844, has been reprinted several times. Some later editions include artwork and biographies that are notably different from those printed in the original edition. While preparing this book, I referred to the 1855 edition printed in Philadelphia by D. Rice and A. N. Hart, a copy of which is in the collection of the State Historical Society of Missouri.

Finally, for more information about White Cloud, see my article "Navigating the White Road: White Cloud's Struggle to Lead the Ioway along the Path of Acculturation," in the January 2005 issue of the *Missouri Historical Review.* To read more about the way artists have portrayed the Ioway leader, see my "Two Portraits, Two Legacies: Anglo American Artists View Chief White Cloud" in the Summer 2004 issue of *Gateway* magazine.

About th

Greg Olson is Curator of E
at the Missouri State Ar